SALES
COMPENSATION
PERSPECTIVES

THE ALEXANDER GROUP

SALES COMPENSATION PERSPECTIVES

THE ALEXANDER GROUP

About Alexander Group

The Alexander Group provides revenue growth consulting services to the world's leading sales, marketing and service organizations. Founded in 1985, Alexander Group combines deep experience, proven methodologies and data-driven insights to help revenue leaders anticipate change, align their go-to-customer resources with company goals and make better informed decisions with one goal in mind—to grow revenue. The Alexander Group has offices in Atlanta, Chicago, London, New York, San Francisco, São Paulo, Scottsdale and Vero Beach.

Our Sales Compensation Consulting Services

As the leading firm in sales compensation design, we help our clients create incentive plans that align selling resources with corporate objectives. The Alexander Group is the recognized thought leader in sales compensation solutions, as widely acknowledged by clients and professional associations.

We have helped thousands of clients, including worldwide sales organizations, realize the full benefits of effective sales compensation programs to reward and recognize high-performing sales resources.

From strategic alignment to design, market pricing and program implementation, we can help with all elements of your sales compensation program.

AGI Press
Sales Compensation Perspectives The Alexander Group

ISBNs:
978-1-7358646-0-0 (print)
978-1-7358646-1-7 (eBook)

This publication is designed to provide accurate and authoritative information in regards to the subject matter covered. It is sold with the understanding that neither the author nor the publisher are engaged in rendering legal, accounting or other professional service. If legal advice or other expert assistance is required, the services of a competent professional person should be sought.

−From a Declaration of Principles Jointly Adopted by a Committee of the American Bar Association and a Committee of Publishers and Associations.

For information about this title or to order other books, contact us at www.alexandergroup.com.

Contents

Editor's Note

Welcome to *Sales Compensation Perspectives!* We are excited to share this invaluable resource featuring 40 sales compensation blogs. The book is an anthology of articles focusing on sales compensation by consultants at the Alexander Group.

This publication classifies articles into five sections to easily locate topics of interest. The sections include Strategic Perspectives, Design Perspectives, Program Management Perspectives, Sales Quota Perspectives and Industry Perspectives.

Special thanks to the many authors who contributed their works: Craig Ackerman, Matt Bartels, Arshad Carim, David Cichelli, Quang Do, Dave Eddleman, Mitchell Edwards, Priya Ghatnekar, Ted Grossman, Avrille Hanzel, Andrew Horvath, Rachel Parrinello, Chris Semain, Kyle Uebelhor and Igor Uroic.

Enjoy!
Lori Feuer, Editor

Strategic Perspectives

Articles in Section

◆

Key Revenue Growth Planning Steps
for Sales Compensation Success

Global Sales Compensation Practices

Is Your Sales Compensation Plan Working?

Keeping Your Sales Roles Crystal Clear

Key Revenue Growth Planning Steps for Sales Compensation Success

Only 19% of the participants in the Alexander Group's annual sales compensation survey reported complete alignment between the sales compensation program and company objectives. Why? Aligned sales compensation plans are dependent on many upstream planning decisions and associated data sets. Unfortunately, many companies fail to deploy a robust business planning process and adequately connect the various data elements.

REVENUE GROWTH PLANNING

A company's business strategy is constantly on the move: new products, new markets, changing buyer behaviors and relentless competitor actions. Companies must continuously review and update their go-to-customer strategies to align to their business strategy. Using the Alexander Group's Revenue Growth Model™, the strategy, structure and management decisions will eventually define the right type of sales compensation plan for each eligible sales job. Where is sales compensation? It is in the ninth—and last—pillar, Compensation & Rewards.

Revenue Growth Model™

BUSINESS PLANNING PROCESSES

Effective revenue growth planning relies on many data-intensive strategy, structure and management planning processes. Upstream data feeds downstream processes. The need for real-time data is a compounding issue. In a recent sales operations survey, 87% of the participants indicated that data integrity/cleanup was a major challenge. Successful companies invest in platform tools to effectively execute their planning processes.

CALL TO ACTION: 7 STEPS

Revenue growth leaders realize that they must employ an effective and efficient revenue planning and execution engine to achieve their revenue growth goals. To realize the full benefit of the sales compensation program, follow these seven mission-critical revenue growth-planning steps.

1. **Build the Revenue Plan.** Be realistic. Be bold. Establish the revenue goal for the operating period. Use historic data, sales segment market research and add gut judgment. This number will inform the expense budget, define investments and establish the revenue goals for the sales compensation plan.

2. **Vet the Sales Expense Budget and Its ROI Impact.** Determine sales force investments, including capacity planning and sales compensation costs.

3. **Use Account Segmentation & Potential to Identify Revenue Opportunities.** Define specific coverage segments based on buyer needs and profitability to maximize productivity at the lowest cost via coverage model, capacity and territory potential.

4. **Analyze Sales Force Capacity.** Deploy the optimal number of resources to maximize revenue within a cost-of-sales budget.

5. **Develop Territories.** Structure balanced territories to equalize quota and sales compensation payout opportunity.

6. **Manage Quota Allocation.** Allocate the revenue plan to each seller: Goals will motivate; payouts will reward.

7. **Adopt Sales Forecasting.** Use ongoing forecasting to inform initial quota setting and mid-year revenue execution corrections.

Companies are constantly looking to improve their internal processes and tools to enable them to execute their go-to-customer models more effectively and efficiently. A singular best-in-class template does not exist. Models will vary based on industry, solution offering, company's growth phase and go-to-customer model. Therefore, detailed planning processes must evolve over time. The key principles and interdependencies of these processes will always exist.

Global Sales Compensation Practices

Global corporate entities deploy numerous and diverse sales resources to serve local markets. Whether the business model features a country, a world-region or a line-of-business configuration, sales teams are usually a "local" solution with local management and local sales practices. This includes local sales compensation programs. When corporate sales compensation designers seek to create uniform sales compensation plans, some local sales leaders will challenge this central approach.

Worldwide sales compensation solutions seem implausible to most local sales leaders. They struggle to understand how uniform sales compensation could apply to their unique situation. A natural reaction from local sales leaders is to ask, "Why?"

- Why does the company need a uniform sales compensation design?

- Why should local sales leaders consider design solutions not tuned to their local market?

- Why should a sales team accept the sales management philosophy from a "foreign" location?

Frankly, pro-global/uniform sales compensation advocates struggle to answer adequately these questions. The following advertised reasons seem weak at best.

- **Simplicity.** This argument suggests that numerous local sales compensation plans are too confusing. Actually, the simplicity test should not be from the perspective of a corporate overseer, but instead from the participant's perspective. If the salesperson understands his or her sales compensation plan, then the plan meets the simplicity test.

- **Too Many Plans.** Again, this is another false objective. The number of plans should equal the number of sales jobs. Local sales leaders correctly devise sales compensation plans to serve local conditions. Experience teaches companies that artificially trying to reduce the number of designs often produces unsatisfactory pay plans for most jobs.

- **Audit and Administration.** A final argument suggests that numerous incentive plans produce an audit and administration conundrum. This is true in some cases. However, since pay programs sit within local sales entities, normal accounting and financial oversight provide satisfactory frameworks for plan management.

The ambitions of central corporate sales compensation planners often find a natural conflict with local sales leaders who seldom see the need for help or direction when designing sales reward programs for their local sales teams.

THE BEST SOLUTION

Local sales leaders are correct: Local sales compensation solutions are best. However, designing effective sales compensation solutions should follow proven, uniform standards. Corporate leaders should document and enforce their sales compensation principles, which embrace best practices for their local sales compensation designers to follow.

Is Your Sales Compensation Plan Working?

Many companies consider changes to the sales compensation program before the start of the new fiscal year. Often, this program becomes out of date due to market dynamics and changes in the company's business and sales strategy. More than 90% of all companies make some changes to their sales compensation program on an annual basis. Is your company experiencing any of the common signs warranting changes to the sales compensation program?

SELLER BEHAVIORS AND SALES COMPENSATION

Do you see any of these seller behaviors at your company?

- **Kingpin Sales Representatives.** Too few salespeople are crushing their number; others are not even close. Finance is concerned.

- **Starving Sales Representatives.** Too many sellers are well behind achieving quota. Some are becoming disenfranchised, checking out or even leaving.

- **Comfortable Sales Representatives.** The current plans don't seem to motivate high performance. The company may be suffering from a nice place to work syndrome.

- **Distrustful Sales Representatives.** They are spending too much time doing shadow accounting to ensure proper credit on sales.

- **Confused Sales Representatives.** They can't understand the plans or the calculations. Many simply give up trying and assume that their manager will take care of them as they do the right thing. (This may or may not be the desired behavior.)

- **Complaining Sales Representatives.** Sales ops/finance work overtime to handle the complaints and exceptions from sales representatives.

- **Happy and Quiet Sales Representatives.** Actually, this is problematic, as well. Sales compensation programs by nature are "noisy." If all is quiet, there is likely something going on.

If your company is experiencing one or more of these seller scenarios, it may be time to evaluate and update your sales compensation program.

SIGNS OF CHANGE

In addition, there are company and market dynamics that signal the need for plan evaluation and redesign, including the following.

- **Mergers or Acquisitions.** Sales compensation programs must align across merged sales forces.

- **New Products.** Launching new products often calls for special sales compensation attention.

- **New Markets or Customer Segments.** Expansion in to new markets or customer segments often warrants plan updates.

- **Route-to-Market Changes.** Shifts in coverage from field to inside, direct to channel, or vice versa call for sales compensation redesign.

- **New Jobs.** Deploying new roles involves ensuring the right sales plans for each job.

- **Changing Jobs.** Changes to the focus or objectives of one or more jobs in the sales force is one of the most common reasons for plan design change.

- **Revenue Model Changes.** When a software company changes from perpetual license deals to subscription deals or from fixed contracts to usage-/consumption-based pricing, it will need to update the sales compensation plans.

- **Changes in Competition.** Competitor advances and moves may warrant sales compensation adjustments.

- **New Executive Leadership.** This may trigger a shift in pay philosophy warranting incentive plan updates.

- **Location Change.** This may necessitate adjustments to pay mix and pay levels.

WHAT WORKS?

What makes sales compensation plans work? Alignment.

It starts with the company strategy and sales strategy. Strategy drives job design. Sales compensation plans follow jobs. There are many variables at play and many voices in the mix. Good sales compensation plans help motivate sellers to achieve success for the customer, the company and their pocketbook. When sales incentives tilt too heavily in one direction, problems arise. For example, tilt them in favor of the company, and sellers may not earn enough. Tilt them in favor of sales representatives, and sales costs might increase while margins decrease. Tilt them too heavily to both the company and salespeople, and customers can be burned.

Sales compensation is the outcome of strategy converted to sales tactics that serve company needs and customer buying preferences.

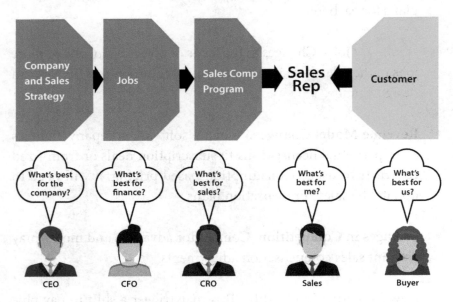

GET READY FOR NEXT YEAR

The first step involves assessing the current sales compensation program. Gather internal data on company objectives, pay philosophy, pay and performance analysis, sales budget, and sales representative and management perspectives. Next, gather market data on pay practices for your industry. Finally, evaluate your plan designs against best practice. Invest the time to conduct a thorough assessment. Doing so provides leadership with needed perspective, so they can determine the design objectives and direction for the new year.

Keeping Your Sales Roles
Crystal Clear

Job clarity is one of the most important elements of employee engagement, driving both job satisfaction and high performance. Although logic indicates that organizations would invest significant time to carefully design and maintain clear roles, this is normally not the case.

CONSIDER THE SALES DEPARTMENT

Here is how the story typically unfolds. It's the middle of the fourth fiscal quarter. The vice president of sales must ensure a strong finish to the year. Meanwhile, the planning efforts for the new fiscal year are well underway. The vice president of sales must devote planning time to determine next year's sales strategy. Oh, did we mention ensuring strong results for the fourth quarter? With next year's sales growth targets and budget decisions quickly coming down from above, the vice president of sales often finds little time to carefully plan next year's strategy beyond making some simplified decisions on coverage model changes–what roles are needed, how many and where? A plan is put together in PowerPoint over the weekend in the 11th month of the year (the vice president of sales knows better than to leave it until the 12th month when there will be zero time). Meanwhile, it's back to the field to rally the troops and help close deals. If lucky, the vice president of sales has a solid sales planning/operations team, which can devote time and attention to the details. Sadly, most have sales operations teams that are overworked, under-resourced and barely able to react to the constant demands for performance data, and territory, quota or sales compensation adjustments. In other cases, HR may come to the rescue and help document job roles. However, HR's ability to help relates directly to how well the company has thought through the sales strategy for the next year and how well HR understands it. Let's just say, there is room for error in this approach.

To make matters worse, the compensation committee is deciding on new sales compensation plans for next fiscal year. The committee makes design decisions on an oversimplified sales strategy and last year's roles.

A better approach. Given the importance of role clarity, sales leaders must either invest the time or get the help they need to design selling roles appropriately. Don't let the important work of job design get "crowded out" by the seemingly more important discussions on strategy or compensation. Jobs are actually the critical fulcrum helping ensure alignment between strategy and compensation.

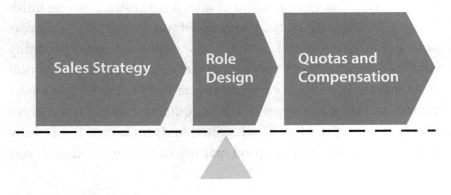

Here are a few tips for how to do this well.

1. **Define Sales Roles in Three Ways: Customers, Products and Processes.** Clearly articulate which customers they should call on, which products they should sell and what process they should follow (and their role in the process); and you will be 70% or more complete.

2. **Be Specific, But Be Concise.** Avoid multipage Word documents that go unread. Put it on one page or one slide. Summarize four things: key accountabilities, key responsibilities, key activities and suggested time allocation.

3. **Use Pictures, Graphs and Colors.** This sounds juvenile, but it's not. Make the job profile attractive. Display a chart to indicate the customers, products or sales process steps that involve reps.

4. **Communicate Roles and Compensation Simultaneously.** Design sales compensation plans around roles. Communicating the roles, in some detail, with the sales compensation program will help ensure alignment and clarity.

5. **Conduct a Sales Force Engagement Survey.** Conduct a survey each year that asks reps to score their job clarity on a scale of one to five. Ask several other questions related to their engagement and their understanding of the sales strategy, their compensation plan, the support available to them, etc. Any score below a four indicates room for improvement.

6. **Use Playbooks to Ensure Role Clarity.** Train first-line sales managers to help model and coach desired behaviors. Your top performers, as you might guess, need the least help. It's the middle of the pack who will benefit the most from this investment. This is the same group of reps who represents the biggest productivity gains for your sales force over the coming year.

Design Perspectives

Articles in Section

◆

Sales Compensation Redefined—Rewarding Customer Outcomes

Is Your Sales Compensation Upside in Overdrive?

Successful Sales Compensation Plan Implementation—A Structured Approach

Sales Compensation Changes: Commit to the Money Not to the Mechanics

Post-Natural Disaster Bust-Boom Strategies

Should You Change Your Sales Compensation Plan for Next Year?
Short Answer: Probably

Sales departments have numerous customer contact jobs: sellers, pre-sales, post-sales, customer support/service, channel management and many others. More than 60 different types of jobs are available for managing customer interactions. Companies configure these jobs to meet the requirements of two variables: product characteristics and buyer needs. Buyers have varying needs, some urgent, others not so much. Some buyers have high product/vendor knowledge; others do not. In addition, the selling tasks of access, persuade and fulfill are different by buyers. Some customers are easy to find, others are not. Some customers are easy to persuade, and others are not. Some customers need extensive customer support, and others do not. Meanwhile, product utility varies by buyer types and application. The competitive environment plus pricing strategies affects the buying equation. Sales force strategic goals may feature one or more objectives: growth, profit, product mix, account types and contract terms. Whew! With this listing, you now have countless permutations of the sales force's goals.

21

Any given B2B sales division will have a few jobs. In some cases, as many as 20 jobs or more. Each of these jobs have a role to help complete the buyer-purchasing journey. The goals for each job are unique to that job. Sales management crafts sales compensation plans to reward achievement of these goals. Each year, sales leadership scans the selling landscape through the lens of the current sales objectives. Any change in product configuration, buyer needs and strategic objectives may alter the goals for one or more sales jobs. As a result, such changes might necessitate a change to the sales compensation plans for those affected jobs. That's why many sales compensation plans change on an annual basis. Our research shows that about 90% of all companies make modifications to the sales compensation plans on an annual basis.

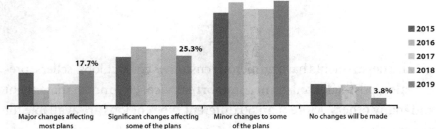

Now that we know sales compensation plans need to be agile, what is necessary to ensure success in a continuously changing sales landscape?

Here are the features of successful annual program redesign efforts.

- **Annual Program Review.** Since it's going to occur anyway, establish and document the annual review and redesign schedule with dates.

- **Governance.** Let people know who is in charge. Establish a governance charter with assigned accountabilities and authorities.

- **Leadership Committees.** Ensure cross-department participation of design changes. Appoint a steering committee to provide executive oversight. Engage a design committee to work through the details of plan revisions.

- **Conditioned Sales Force.** Sales leadership needs to communicate to the sales force that plan revisions are a normal part of sales effectiveness efforts.

- **Automation and Administration.** Ensure program automation and administration protocols can record performance and process payments.

The takeaway: Sales management must align the sales compensation plan within the context of buyers, products and selling strategies. Make the annual sales compensation review process a repeatable and well-tuned effort.

5 Simple Rules for Sales Compensation Plans

*D*oes the "best" sales compensation solution exist? Sales leaders universally believe sales compensation drives sales outcomes. Easy enough. Is there a single best way to structure sales compensation plans? Unfortunately, not. Follow these five rules to configure the ideal sales compensation plan for your team.

Rule No. 1: Determine If the Job is a Producer or a Sales Representative. There are two types of sellers: producers and sales representatives. Producers "own" their book of business and they "split" the revenue with the "house." Examples include real estate agents, stockbrokers, traders and life insurance agents. Pay the industry commission rate—expand and contract headcount based on market activity. Sales representatives have a market target total compensation split into a base component and incentive opportunity with upside earning potential for exceptional performance. Select performance measures to match fiscal and sales objectives. Change annually as necessary. Use a calculated commission rate if territories are equal; use a bonus formula to reward quota achievement performance when territories are dissimilar in size.

Rule No. 2: Use One Sales Compensation Plan per Job. Sales compensation plans work best when the incentive plan "speaks" to the salesperson. This occurs when the target pay is competitive and performance measures align with their assigned duties. These two conditions justify the need for unique sales compensation plans per job. Use company sales compensation principles to keep the underlying framework the same for all jobs, but still accommodate unique target pay and performance measures per job.

Rule No. 3: Balance Risk and Reward. After determining the target total compensation for the job, split this amount into a base salary and incentive element. A 70/30 pay mix allocates 70% of the target total compensation to base salary and 30% to target incentive. Pay mixes vary from 50/50 to 85/15. Use a more aggressive pay mix for "high influence" sales jobs and a less aggressive pay mix for "lower influence" sales jobs. Ensure that the best performers—the 90th percentile of performance—can earn three times the target incentive. Don't cap the plan. Allow 10% to exceed this 3x upside earning target.

Rule No. 4: Pick the Right Measures. Use no more than three measures. Ensure one of the measures is a sales production measure. Allocate the most incentive opportunity to the production measure. Do not select measures the salesperson cannot influence. Do not use incentive dollars to reward activities or compliance. Avoid using management by objective (MBO) measures except for major account sellers.

Rule No. 5: Delineate Sales Crediting. Pay sales personnel for successful sales persuasion. Do not pay for persuasion twice; pay upfront for recurring revenue, but do not provide future credit when no additional persuasion is necessary. Credit supervisors with subordinate sales success. Carefully evaluate any "shared" or "double" crediting to ensure the seller is getting the proper allocation of sales credit results. Finally, sales credit timing should occur when the company no longer wants the seller to think about the order. The most common practice is to credit the sale at invoice/ship timing.

The "best" sales compensation plan rewards sales success, motivates sellers and follows these simple rules: job type, number of plans, risk/reward balance, the right measures and the right sales crediting.

Reprinted with permission from McGraw-Hill's BusinessBlog. Read more about sales compensation plans in Compensating the Sales Force by David Cichelli.

How to Assess Your Sales Compensation Program

Now that it's close to the end of the fiscal year, it's time to ask the question, "Does our sales compensation plan need updated for the next fiscal year?" Begin soon, if you plan to make changes to the sales compensation program for the next fiscal year. Where do you start? Here is brief summary of how to assess your sales compensation program and determine your program goals and design priorities for next year.

It's all about alignment. Sales compensation plans work properly when they align in three important ways: 1) to your business and sales strategy, 2) to your compensation design principles and 3) to the market in which you compete for sales talent.

Strategic Alignment. Are the company's business and sales strategies changing as you look toward next year? If the sales strategy is changing (target customers, channels, sales process, product/services), then most likely the sales roles need updating. Start by confirming the go-to-market strategy for next fiscal year. Are you deploying new channels or roles? The final "product" from this exercise is a set of one-page job profiles outlining the core responsibilities, accountabilities, activities and time profile for each role. These roles tie to the sales compensation plans.

Principle Alignment. Follow the company's sales compensation principles. Do you have a set of guiding principles? It's much easier to evaluate your compensation plans when you know the true north for your company. Are you a nice place to work or do you want to "feed the eagles, starve the turkeys"? Setting your philosophy will determine the kind of sales culture you foster. Next, analyze your pay, performance and plan designs. How many reps are hitting quota? What is the performance distribution? At this stage, evaluate both the compensation plans and supporting programs such as territory designs and quotas. Sometimes the plans are fine, but the quotas or territories need better alignment to the roles.

Market Alignment. How do the pay levels compare to labor market competitors? Most companies benchmark base salary and target total compensation (TTC) and there are several survey houses that offer good pay data. However, this alone will not reveal potential differences in earning opportunity for high performers. Evaluating other aspects of the plan design, including the use of thresholds, accelerators, crediting rules, plan complexity, performance period and frequency of payment (to name a few), will help ensure that your compensation plans help attract and not detract top sales talent. Benchmarks on plan design are more difficult to find.

Worth the Investment. It is worth dedicating time, resources and budget to properly evaluate and update your sales compensation program every year. The typical company spends 20 cents of every dollar on the sales force. Nearly half of this goes to sales compensation. The impact of good sales compensation plans is real–and often translates into productivity gains of 1% to 5% or more.

Are Sales Compensation Costs Variable? Yes, No and Yes

A re sales compensation costs variable for the company? Here is the short answer: For income producers, the answer is yes. For sales representatives, the answer is no. However, what about the sales personnel themselves? Regardless of seller category—income producer versus sales representative—the answer is yes. Sales compensation is a variable pay plan for the participants. Wait. What?

To begin, we have to confirm there are two types of sellers: 1) income producers and 2) sales representatives. Income producers are (or should be) paid full commission. They create value by nurturing buyer relationships and connections. Often, the products are commodity and ubiquitous. Producers split income transactions with the house. Think real estate agents, financial advisers, traders, mortgage origination personnel, manufacturing reps, stockbrokers and life insurance agents. Their costs are fully variable for the company: The more the producers sell, the more they are paid; the less they sell, the less they are paid. Note: While the payouts are variable, the payout rate is the same for all sellers.

Meanwhile, sales representatives are employees who sell their company's unique configuration of products. Management defines sales objectives. They receive pay for persuasion success. Sales representatives have a target total pay amount. This amount is split between a base pay element and a target incentive amount. This ratio is the pay mix. The total of the at-risk target incentive amounts creates the budget of incentive payments. As such, sales personnel are funding their own incentive program. The low performers are paying the high performers. Correctly assigned quotas ensure costs to the company are not variable. At the end of the year, the total payouts should approximate the total of at-risk target incentive amounts. The overall costs to the company are not variable.

However, payouts are fully variable to the individual seller. For both seller categories, the better sellers earn more than the lower performing sellers do.

Are sales incentive costs variable for the company? For income producers, yes. For sales representatives, no. For all sellers, (ouch) yes.

A RECENT QUESTION

Question: It takes us a long time to get sales data on indirect transactions. Is there a best practice between crediting upon receipt or crediting before shipment? We currently do this and it is very process intensive and inefficient; however, we do not know if there are other options out there.

Answer: Pay on sales-out data! Yes, it takes a long time to get accurate data from channel partners. However, you have no other choice. You would not want to pay on sales-in data to the partner...this can cause "loading of the channel"—not a desirable outcome. Sorry, no easy solution around the time delay for this information. There are companies that gather this information from distributors and sell it back to manufacturers.

The Alexander Group has been conducting sales compensation trends and practice surveys since 2003. Here is a look at one interesting finding.

WHAT PERCENT OF COMPANIES HAVE A LEGAL ISSUE WITH THEIR SALES COMPENSATION PLAN?

This question defines the threshold of a legal issue as follows: A lawyer has written a letter on behalf of a seller claiming unfair treatment. This question appeared in our surveys five times over the last 20 years, and the answer is remarkably consistent:

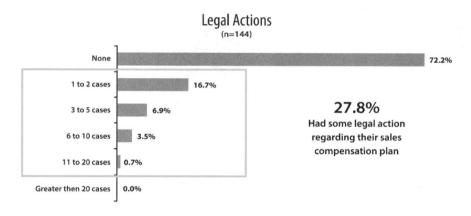

Sales Compensation:
Target Total Compensation

How should you price your sales jobs? Use these guidelines to set and manage pay levels for all your sales compensation eligible jobs.

- Define a clear and consistent target market pay philosophy.

- Set target total compensation (TTC) at the appropriate percentile to attract and retain the right talent required by the sales organization to execute its strategy.

- Benchmark to the right roles based upon job content; use internal equity when no market benchmark exists.

- Benchmark to a select group of companies based upon market competitors, talent competition and similar sales motions.

Most companies leverage the following target pay-level practices.

- **Pay Philosophy.** The most common practice is to set the pay philosophy at the 50th percentile of a firm's target market. Some companies willing to pay more for high caliber talent will set their pay levels at the 60th or 75th percentile of their market.

- **Market Pay Surveys.** Most companies purchase one to three surveys to benchmark and set pay levels for their jobs. If using multiple surveys, do not weight or average results, because it will most likely double count data from some participating companies.

- **Target Market.** To ensure ample n-counts within all survey jobs/ job levels by country, companies should define 20 to 30 companies within each market pay survey as their target market. This list should include both product and talent competitors. When needed, expand the definition to include companies with similar sales motions.

- **TTC Pay Level Setting Methodology.** The best practice is to set the TTC level and then apply appropriate pay mix to calculate base salary and target incentive. See the pay-level setting methodology in Figure 1.

- **Pay Mix Methodology.** A fixed pay mix methodology places all incumbents on the same pay mix regardless of their TTC level. This methodology provides all incumbents with the same target incentive and different base salaries/pay mixes. Use fixed pay mixes when pay varies widely within each job level and fixed target incentives when variations are narrow.

- **TTC Pay Ranges.** Determine the appropriate pay range above and below the pay level midpoint based on degree of job content variance. Minimize pay gaps and pay overlap between job levels. The most common practice is to use a pay range between +/- 10% to 20%. However, some companies will decrease the range for higher job/pay levels to reduce the pay overlap between levels. In Figure 1, the example TTC pay ranges show a 20% range above and below the midpoint.

- **Geographic Pay Differentials.** Some companies vary pay levels by geographic locations to accommodate cost of labor/living differences. Set differentials for lower paying jobs where the geographic location has significant impact on pay levels. Set national pay levels (no differentials) for higher paying jobs where job mobility is more common and the pay range can accommodate geographic location differences.

Compa-Ratio. To benchmark your current practices, calculate the compa-ratio by dividing each employee's pay level by the pay structure midpoint. Healthy compa-ratios vary depending on the range—it should be between .8 and 1.2 for a 20% pay range spread. See the compa-ratio example in Figure 1.

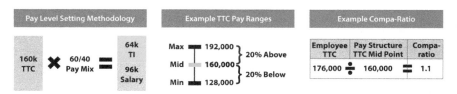

Figure 1

MARKET DATA INTERPRETATION NOTES

Market data can be misleading due to how companies map and submit their data for each job level. It is common for n-counts to vary dramatically by levels, making data for some levels suspect. Sometimes higher job levels will have lower pay levels. Therefore, just looking at one data point (e.g., the 50th percentile) for specific job levels can be misleading. Best practice is to chart multiple percentiles for all job levels. Figure 2 graphically displays overall market practices to inform final pay level decisions. For example, the company had only three job levels and paid at the 50th percentile. However, by analyzing how the company pays all five of the job levels, as well as multiple percentiles (25th, 50th and the 75th), the company was able to set a structure to accommodate most of the market.

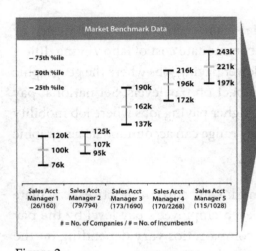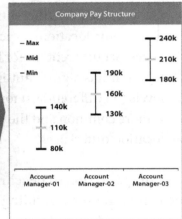

Figure 2

Focusing Selling Effort
on the New Product

At a recent roundtable, chief financial officers expressed concern about the cost of sales compensation. "It should be impossible for reps to have a great year if the company has a bad year," one CFO shared.

Sound familiar? However, when asked about their "burning" sales compensation issues, one topic seemed to represent a common strategic theme among the group: "How can we focus selling efforts on new products?"

As is often the case when reps are not meeting new product goals, the sales compensation program is the first to blame. Changing the compensation plan is a viable solution in some cases. For example, carving out a separate measure for the new product or creating a product mix objective can drive rep focus. However, plan design changes will only help under certain circumstances. Before jumping to sales compensation for the answer, executives should first consider the following three questions.

1. How similar is the buyer for the new product *(compared to the core product)?*

2. How similar is the sales process for the new product *(compared to the core product)?*

3. How well do customers understand the new product *(compared to the core product)?*

The answers to these questions address the more fundamental question: "Can my existing sales force successfully sell the new product?" If the new products are bought by the same customer and level of buyer with a similar sales process (sales cycle length, complexity) and the new product has a similar level of market awareness or maturity as the core, then it's reasonable to expect the existing sales reps can successfully sell the new product. In these instances, redesigning the sales compensation plan may be the answer. However, the more drastic the differences between the new product and the core product, the more drastic the solution required to achieve the right sales focus on the new product.

Consider the following simple schematic outlining a continuum of solutions based on the degree of differences:

The right solution can range from a simple adjustment to the current compensation plan to launching a completely separate sales force. Even if the differences are small, the sales force may require new training and coaching in conjunction with the right incentives. Drastically different products usually will not get the necessary selling focus from training and new incentive plans. Job design and coverage model changes are necessary. This usually comes at a higher cost. It's cheaper to just add more products to the same seller's bag. However, if the product is not getting the needed attention, it requires more investment. Understanding what level of investment is required can seem like a guessing game. The bigger the investment, the bigger the risk of failure.

What's the key takeaway? When faced with challenges selling the new product, leaders should not rush to "fix" the compensation plan. Doing so can result in wasted time and money on product incentives and rep training that will not improve new product sales. A broader evaluation focused on the three key questions outlined earlier is a better starting point. Leadership must collaborate–product development, marketing, finance and sales–to plan the best course of action.

Sales Compensation Plan
Eligibility

Which jobs should be eligible to participate in the company's sales compensation plan? Use these guidelines to establish eligibility criteria at your company.

The most common eligibility guidelines include the following details; the primary job must meet all three of the following criteria:

1. Significant customer or partner contact

2. Customer/partner persuasion to buy/resell company offerings

3. Clear and quantifiable sales goals

What about other jobs that have customer contact? Should they be eligible to participate in the sales compensation program? What about field marketing jobs, customer success personnel and lead generation roles? What about sales support personnel such as sales administration, sales operations and in-bound order entry?

CALIBRATING THE ELIGIBILITY CRITERIA

Companies can narrow or widen the eligibility criteria.
Example guidelines that narrow the criteria include:

- Specific time allocation focused on selling (e.g., 80% of time)

- Ability to measure and track sales goals

- Clear tie of revenue to influence/persuasion

- Sales quota responsibility

- Sales territory assignment

Example guidelines that widen the criteria include:

- Progress an individual opportunity to qualification status (includes lead generation representatives)

- Persuade the customer to act in a positive financial benefit (includes business development roles focused on reducing costs)

- Persuade the stakeholder to adopt or use company offering (includes customer success representatives)

- Responsible for optimizing revenue (includes digital media campaign optimization roles)

- Persuade stakeholders to buy company offerings via direct contact or one-to-many campaigns (includes digital/online store managers)

A DETAILED LOOK AT PERSUASION CRITERIA

Industry professionals use the word persuasion a lot. Why? The most important asset in your sales organization is your sellers' time spent persuading the customer to buy your product and consequently generating revenue. Companies gear the sales compensation plan to pay those sales representatives for their persuasion activities. Therefore, persuasion is a key element to many sales compensation design components, eligibility being a primary one. Be aware . . . many industries/sales models have additional persuasion events besides closing a contract, including obtaining technical sign-off, progressing an opportunity and driving adoption/usage.

PLAN TYPE

Eligibility includes identifying the correct plan type, too. The most common types of sales compensation plans are as follows:

- **Unit Rate Plan.** Companies use this plan for agents (e.g., real estate agents, independent agents and brokers) where the market dictates the commission rate. A test for agents is whether they can take their business with them if they leave the company.

- **3x Uncapped.** This plan works best for sales roles that represent the company's unique products and services. The seller represents the company's products. Sellers earn a base salary and a target incentive based on market labor rates. Target incentive is pay-at-risk and not paid until the seller achieves a sales goal. Express the mix between base salary and target incentive as a percent of the target total compensation (TTC) (e.g., 60/40 means 60% of TTC is base salary, and 40% of TTC is target incentive). For every dollar at risk, sellers are eligible for three times the target incentive in upside pay that is uncapped (thus, 3x uncapped).

- **2x Capped.** Companies use this plan for executive programs, consumer packaged goods sellers and some professional service roles. Sellers receive a base salary and an at-risk target incentive based on market labor rates. Express the target incentive as a percent of the base salary. For every dollar at risk, sellers are eligible for two times their target incentive in upside pay, and their upside is capped (thus, 2x capped).

SALES COMPENSATION PLAN TYPES

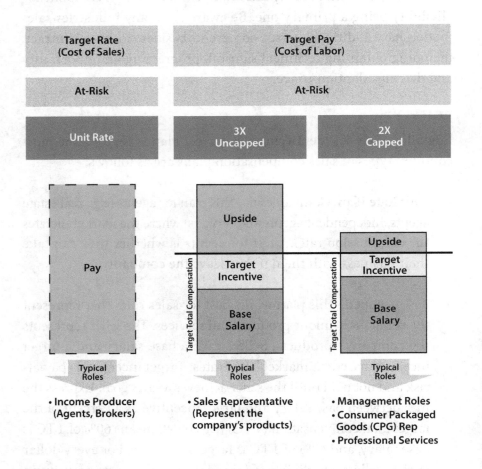

MISUSE OF SALES COMPENSATION PLANS FOR NON-SALES ROLES

A common mistake is to provide non-sales roles with a sales compensation plan. This is particularly acute when companies do not have corporate bonus plans for non-sellers. Some sales leaders will desire to put customer service, marketing, sales support/coordinators, sales operations, deal desk and other roles into the sales compensation program as they seek to recognize and reward performance. However, pay-at-risk plans require the incumbent to have significant impact on outcomes. It is ill-advised to subject these jobs to downside earnings when their efforts cannot directly drive outcomes.

ELIGIBILITY APPLICATION NOTES

There are many guidelines, concepts, frameworks and practices when it comes to sales compensation plan eligibility. Each company should develop its own guidelines that align to its specific philosophies and principles. Companies should determine plan eligibility at the job and not the incumbent level. When developing a new job, sales should work with HR to confirm the job role and responsibilities and whether or not it adheres to company eligibility guidelines. Eligibility guidelines do not always need to align to market practice; however, companies do need to consistently apply these guidelines and support the overall philosophy of the company. When building out eligibility criteria, sales organizations must articulate how each criterion will impact current/future role eligibility, so leaders understand the impact of their decisions.

Sales Compensation Redefined— Rewarding Customer Outcomes

Traditional sales compensation plans are clearly one-sided. Simply put, pay plans reward sales personnel for increasing the selling company's sales results, not for meeting the customers' needs. More elaborate sales compensation pay programs reward refined measures such as product mix, profit/price attainment or purchasing continuity while all serving the same master—the selling company. As such, these are one-sided reward systems; they serve the selling company, but not the customer.

What about the value delivered to customers? Should companies reward sales personnel for customer outcomes? Few, if any, pay programs reward for customer success. Why not? Is it possible? Should companies consider it?

THE HOLY GRAIL OF CUSTOMER SUCCESS

The dividing line between corporate rhetoric and actual practice begins with the phrase, "We are here to serve our customers," yet ends with a pay program, which rewards for improving the company's sales results. No gulf is wider than the distance between this "customer do-good" rhetoric and the actual pay program practice. Admittedly, aligning a company's objectives and its customers' success is an elusive goal. Regardless, the reward system—sell more—speaks louder than any "customer-first" philosophy of meeting and exceeding customer needs.

An illustration from the fitness center industry provides a stark example of this paradox. A national fitness center company pays its sales personnel to sign up new customers in long-term contracts with automatic monthly payments. In fact, the pricing model significantly discourages one-time upfront payments. Monthly payments have proven more "sticky" than one-time payments. Many people simply continue to have their bank account debited without realizing the cumulative impact of these monthly payments. Re-signing a customer to a long-term contract with another upfront payment has proven much more difficult than the relentless (seemingly insignificant) automatic monthly payments. The customer is paying and paying. Not a bad outcome if the customer is using the fitness center. That's a big "if." It's well known in the fitness business that few customers continue to use the fitness center after the initial sign-up period. Many terminate their contracts, or worse, let the automatic payments continue without using the fitness center. As expected, the arrival of each new year sees the greatest gain in membership from the "I've-got-to-get-in-shape-tribe." Sadly, they quickly give up and stop going to the gym. This revolving-door model eventually burns through the available local customer base.

Consider this: What if the reward system is tied to fitness center usage, not just continuing payments? It would significantly change the complexion of the fitness industry with greater emphasis on member indoctrination, affiliation, tracking and program support. And, what if, customer goal outcomes (weight loss, strength, endurance and health gains) were part of this reward system? Needless to say, the fitness business would be something more than discouraged newbies passing through the home of a few hardcore fitness addicts.

An additional example is visible in the airline industry: Airlines are fastidious about measuring airplane on-time performance. They use classic business-process optimization methods to improve on-time performance of airplanes. Although airplanes have a schedule to meet, they are not paying for the service—passengers are. Consider this, what if the airlines measured the extent of delay for passengers on a weighted usage basis? In other words, all flyers will have a cumulative annual total of minutes delayed, but a frequent flyer will have a higher weighted delay index. In other words, planes have no clocks; passengers do. Reducing cumulative passenger delay for the most frequent high-revenue producing flyers might change the investments regarding on-time performance. Heavy business routes would get the needed attention for on-time performance before leisure travel routing.

THE FALSE PROMISE OF CUSTOMER SERVICE MEASURES

Many companies have sought to measure customer satisfaction, retention or promotion with customer feedback surveys. Unfortunately, most surveys ask the wrong question, "How are we doing?" Not, "how are you (the customer) doing?" Nothing illustrates this better than the annoying practice of auto dealer service managers begging customers not to rate them anything less than 10 on a 1 to 10 scale of satisfaction. Shameful. Customer satisfaction surveys, mystery shopper results and net promoter scores all suffer from the same myopic focus on the selling company's performance and not on the customers' outcomes.

REWARDING CUSTOMER OUTCOMES

As radical as it might sound, let's consider the following customer outcomes as potential reward measures for sellers:

- **Return on Investment (ROI).** What was the ROI of the customer's purchase of the company's product? What benefit did it get?

- **Sales Growth.** Did the customer's sales growth improve from purchasing the product?

- **Productivity Improvement.** Did the customers' productivity improve? Did production costs go down?

- **Customer-Defined Success Measures.** Does the pay program reward customer-defined measures? Has the seller, the company, asked the customers what they define as success?

Expected retorts of measuring customer success might include too costly, too unreasonable and too inexact. However, as a hypothesis, relentless digging into customer outcomes will reveal new measures—measures that might augment traditional measures of seller success. A company will surprise and delight its customers if it informs them that seller rewards are tied to their success. A remarkable feat of shrinking the divide between hollow customer-centric rhetoric and seller reward systems will occur. Surely, a prescription for market success!

Is Your Sales Compensation Upside in Overdrive?

As with any sales compensation program, balancing the need to provide competitive incentives and manage costs can be difficult to get right. One area that can cause headaches is "upside," which is the term given to payments made for above-goal performance. Getting it right can spur talented sellers into over-goal performance; getting it wrong can bleed your sales compensation budget dry. Setting upside incorrectly can lead to negative consequences whether it is set too high or too low. Low upside, for example, can significantly affect motivation, morale and retention of talented sellers. However, upside that is set too high results in sales compensation overpayments. Here are three examples that illustrate overpayment.

Example No. 1: Small Quota With High Upside. In some declining revenue industries, such as integrated media, quota sizes have declined over time and may be causing increased costs. Consider the following example of a local territory representative with a $300K quota size and a $30K target incentive. If the plan is designed to pay 3x target incentive at 120% performance (i.e., excellence point: the performance level where we expect the top 10% of sellers to achieve and pay full upside), all incremental revenue above goal will be paid to the sales representative. Clearly, this plan would not be affordable.

Be careful to balance plan upside with appropriate quota sizes. In this example, either the upside needs reduced or the quota needs to be increased.

Example No. 2: Incorrect Excellence Point. The Alexander Group recently worked with a company that set its excellence point for a new revenue stream at 150% targeting 3x leverage. Analysis of historical performance showed that the excellence point should have been set at 190% plus. Not only did this miscalculation lead to significant overpayments as people outperformed expectations, it also indicated a larger issue with quota setting.

To reduce the financial exposure of new products, consider including a cap or decelerator. Alternatively, ensure a thorough analysis goes into determining quotas and excellence points.

Example No. 3: High Compensation Cost of Sales. Compensation cost of sales (CCOS) is a metric that organizations use to determine the sales compensation costs as a percentage of revenue. To calculate, simply sum up all the total cash sales compensation components (base salary, variable incentive and spiffs) and divide by total revenue. As the excellence point decreases and the upside amount increases, the CCOS will invariably increase.

The CCOS for each role within a company can vary significantly. In integrated media, local territory representatives can have a CCOS between 15% and 20% due to their smaller quota sizes. Strategic representatives, on the other hand, will have a CCOS less than 5%.

To avoid an unnecessarily high CCOS, conducting comprehensive modeling under different performance scenarios is essential once plan designs are complete.

Avoiding these pitfalls can lead to a reduction in the CCOS and more efficient use of the sales compensation budget. The following chart shows the modeled impact on a group of 40 sellers from correctly setting the excellence point with historical data.

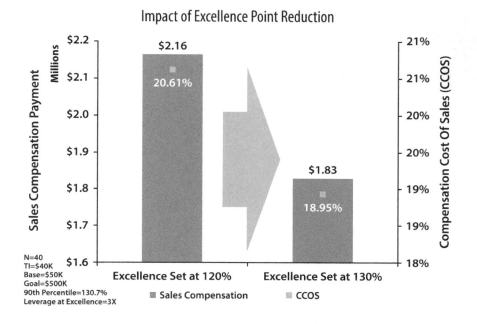

Impact of Excellence Point Reduction

Successful Sales Compensation
Plan Implementation
A Structured Approach

The approaching end of the fiscal year kicks off sales compensation planning for the next fiscal year. This annual exercise presents many potential challenges. World-class sales organizations begin the process of assessing their current sales compensation plans in order to determine if changes are necessary and to align with the company's evolving sales strategy. If there are any changes to the sales compensation plans, the organization ensures that it has a clear plan to communicate and implement the new plans. Implementation success begins with the following five key areas.

1. **Communication.** Communication is an essential component to sales compensation plan adoption. To ensure the organization embraces the sales compensation plans, designers should establish a communication cadence, which is clear, concise and frequent.

2. **Alignment.** Sales compensation plan design starts with gaining a clear picture of the job roles and responsibilities. Sales compensation plans are a way to communicate to the sellers what behaviors the organization wants to reward. Plan designers need to be sure that all changes align to job responsibilities that may have evolved.

3. **Motivation.** While plan designers ensure that the plans will provide sales compensation for sales performance, the communication strategy needs to communicate clearly how sellers can earn incentive through the new program.

4. **Measures.** Sales compensation plans should include performance measures that the seller has the ability to impact. Additionally, any performance measures included in the plan should be well defined.

5. **Quotas.** Organizations can design what they perceive to be the best sales compensation plan, but the success relies on the ability to set achievable sales goals. Organizations need to have sound quota-setting practices to ensure that the sales compensation plan functions as intended. In order to get quota setting right, sales leaders should expect to spend time and effort to allocate goals appropriately.

ROADBLOCKS

There can be a few roadblocks along the way, as well. A structured implementation plan that considers potential roadblocks is critical to ensure adoption into the organization.

Here are four key roadblocks and ways around them that plan designers should consider.

- **Roadblock No. 1: Attachment to Old Plan.** When sales organizations do not make changes or updates to the plan regularly, sellers can become attached emotionally to the old plan and may perceive any change as negative. **Solution:** Organizations should communicate regularly on the reason for change and the potential impact of the plan changes on sales. Plan communication materials should provide sellers with examples of new incentive calculations to promote transparency and understanding.

- **Roadblock No. 2: Inertia.** Sellers who don't understand new expectations. **Solution:** Make sure that sellers understand what the new selling expectations are; otherwise, the sales compensation plans will not serve their intended purpose. The implementation plan should also seek to reacquaint sellers with their job roles and responsibilities at a high level.

- **Roadblock No. 3: Clarity.** Plans that include performance measures that are unmeasurable. **Solution:** Achievement on performance measures that cannot be backed by accurate data leaves room for subjectivity. Sellers should be able to trust the data source that leads to their sales incentive compensation. Without this, the integrity of the sales compensation plan can be lost.

- **Roadblock No. 4: Complexity.** Plans that include overcomplicated plan mechanics. **Solution:** Design sales compensation plans in a way that sellers can easily calculate their incentive payments based on their performance. If sellers cannot understand plan mechanics, there is a risk they will not be motivated to drive results since they won't understand how their performance translates into sales compensation dollars.

As designers begin their planning strategy, successful implementation will depend on having clear directions and a solid end goal. To avoid potential roadblocks during the sales compensation plan rollout, plan designers should provide a detailed rollout plan for implementation, including manager training and clear plan documentation.

Sales Compensation Changes: Commit to the Money Not to the Mechanics

What is the best way to tell the sales force you are changing their sales compensation plan?

Sales compensation plans need to change if either one of these two variables change: company selling objectives or buyer purchasing preferences. These continually moving forces—product/company ambitions and buyer preferences—cause changes to sales job accountabilities. Whenever these accountabilities change, the sales compensation plan may need to change as well. A sales compensation plan could function for numerous years without revisions or updates. Eventually, however, underlying conditions driven by changes to product strategy or buyer preferences will require a realignment of selling accountabilities and thus the sales compensation plan.

Oops, we just bumped into an often-heard objection: "You can't change the sales compensation plan, it will upset the sellers." We have heard this statement before and it's legitimate. We do not want to distract or upset the sellers. However, the plans need to change. What is the change-management solution to address this dilemma?

Let's solve this problem by committing to the money not to the mechanics.

Most sales compensation plans have an effective date—the start of the fiscal year; and an expiration date—the last day of the fiscal year. This allows for needed annual changes. However, some companies are reluctant to make changes for fear of upsetting the sales force. This is particularly true of companies that have had few changes to the sales compensation plan in the previous years.

The origins of "fear of change" rest with the history of how sales management introduced the current pay plan. A common mistake is to present the pay plan as a base plus an incentive formula. "Welcome sales force, we are here to describe your new incentive plan for next year. In addition to your base pay, you will earn incentives based on this formula mechanic." The presentation continues with a table of the incentive formula and several incentive calculation illustrations. This is well and good. However, the next time you need to change the formula to reflect a new selling reality, changing the formula is going to raise questions and, in some cases, suspicions. "Why the change?" "Are you trying to reduce my incentive earnings?"

Seldom do companies wish to reduce sellers' earnings. Instead, they often seek to redirect sellers' efforts to new goals: new products, new accounts, profitability and other strategic objectives. Sometimes, buyers shift their purchases. For example, to the e-channel affecting sales crediting practices. These changes will require adjustments to the pay plan.

Here is how to introduce correctly the new sales compensation plan.

"Welcome sellers! We are here to talk about the revised sales compensation plan for next year. Your base pay levels will continue, including the regular annual review. Our budget for sales compensation has increased from last year. You will have increased earning opportunities as a result of this x% increase. (Or..."We are continuing with our sales compensation budget from last year for this year.") As we do each year, we reexamined our sales priorities to ensure alignment between our strategic objectives and our buyers' needs. We reformulated our plans to reflect these fiscal-year objectives. Let's take a close look at the new plan design...!"

As you move forward with the new sales objectives, you have assured the sales force "the money is still there!"

Commit to the money not to the mechanics!

Post-Natural Disaster Bust-Boom Strategies

After a natural disaster, manufacturers often experience a period of bust and boom. Fluctuation in sales activity emerges as each impacted region begins to recover and eventually rebuild. This is the time for manufacturing sales leaders to review their sales incentive compensation programs and to adjust to align with new market conditions. After monitoring and gaining insights into the market environment, sales leadership can utilize the following strategies to reassess the sales impact following a natural disaster.

Organizations with *limited* insight into the extent of future sales fluctuations will benefit from the following four strategies:

1. **Leave the Current Plan in Place.** Sales management may elect to make no changes to the current sales incentive compensation structure, especially when it is difficult to forecast sales. They may elect to leave the plan in place for the remainder of the year and revisit quotas and sales compensation for the following year.

Pro: Keeping the plan "as-is" is a simple solution, which does not require any additional communication or change management.

Con: There is uncertainty of what the financial impact of the sales compensation plan will be. Incentive payments could be either significantly higher or lower than anticipated.

2. **Adjust Quotas.** Management may elect to modify current sellers' quotas mid-year.

    Pro: Adjusting quotas up or down while keeping the plan structure will attempt to fit an existing pay curve to the new situation and keep the same performance distribution under the new reality.

    Con: If the changes in quota are not accurate, there is the potential for significant overpayment for results. On the other hand, if the quotas are unattainable, sellers may feel alienated due to loss of hope.

3. **Adjust Thresholds.** Decreased thresholds will lead to sellers earning incentive sooner.

    Pro: Sellers will get "into the money" sooner than they would have under the old plan.

    Con: Decreasing the threshold might make the plan more expensive to administer.

4. **Implement a "Make Whole Provision."** Consider suspending the current plan, pay sellers the target incentive for their year and cap the plan.

    Pro: Under this provision, sellers will benefit from payment of their full incentive amount at target. An added bonus: Sellers will move towards a team mentality.

    Con: This provision will cap the incentive payments at target, which will provide no upside payments for sellers who outperformed targets for the period.

Companies whose management has a complete *lack of insight* into quotas will likely benefit from the following additional alternative.

5. **Devise an Alternate Sales Compensation Program.** Management may elect to pay sellers sales incentive compensation on an alternate program that does not rely on sales results. Measures for this plan would include key performance indicators (KPIs). Sellers would still have the ability to earn sales incentive compensation without relying on sales results.

    Pro: This plan eliminates reliance on sound quota setting in an uncertain market environment.

    Con: Changes to the plan mid-year can potentially confuse sellers. The organization will have to lay out clearly a communication strategy.

Regardless of which route an organization decides to choose, it is important for companies to react with a clear understanding of what is happening in the marketplace. Evidence from previous natural disasters shows a dip in sales and then a significant uptick due to the boom in construction. Manufacturing sales organizations need to ensure that they do a full plan evaluation six months following these changes to confirm the plan is still in line with market factors.

Program Management Perspectives

Articles in Section

◆

Sales Compensation Program Management:
Not Just for Big Complex Companies

Effective Sales Compensation Design: Using Sales
Compensation Principles

Platform Jobs: The Secret to Manage Sales Comp
in Big Companies

Effective Governance: Making Sales Compensation Successful

Create Design Goalposts to Manage Sales Compensation
Plan Consistency

Sales Compensation Goalposts—Global Solution Case Study

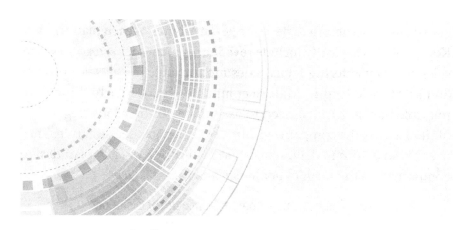

Sales Compensation
Program Management:
Not Just for Big Complex Companies

There's more to managing sales compensation plans than simply designing and rolling the plans out on time—even for small companies. Both small and big best-in-class companies should invest in foundational program management practices. How can companies big and small effectively scale their sales compensation programs as they grow? A good start begins by deploying the following management practices.

PLATFORM JOBS: NONE → CLASSIFICATION STRUCTURE → PLATFORM JOB DECISION TREE

Startup companies generally have a small set of key sales jobs. They don't require a sophisticated job taxonomy structure. As companies grow, the number and types of jobs proliferate. HR titles, business card titles and plan titles become outdated and disconnected. Issues arise such as out-of-date job descriptions, inappropriate pay levels and misaligned sales compensation plans. Scaling companies build a classification structure to describe key attributes of each platform job. Key attributes typically include revenue segment focus, territory size, sales strategy, offering focus, sales motion, role in the sales process and sales cycle length. Mature companies (particularly those with multiple business units) need to assimilate all their jobs (regardless of title) across the company within a platform job decision tree. They use this structure to drive consistent application of each plan design component in the form of goalposts (discussed later).

Sales Compensation Program Management Evolution

Company Size

		Startup	Scaling	Mature
Platform Jobs	Groupings of roles performing similar duties based on a list of specific attributes; structured methodology to classify, rationalize and manage all sales jobs	○	◑	●
Philosophies/ Principles/ Guidelines	Set of sales compensation values and detailed guidelines for each plan design component based on the company's pay philosophies and best-in-class market practices	◑	●	●
Goalposts	Application of component guidelines to each specific platform job in the form of acceptable ranges	○	○	●
Process	Activities, timeline and owners across the end-to-end process (Plan, Design, Implement, Administer, Assess and Manage)	◔	◑	●
Governance	Defined responsibilities by function/job throughout the end-to-end process, including escalation pathways	◔	◑	●

Low Application ○ ◔ ◑ ◕ ● High Application

PHILOSOPHIES/PRINCIPLES/COMPONENT GUIDELINES: PHILOSOPHIES/PRINCIPLES → COMPONENT GUIDELINES

Regardless of company size, all companies must define their pay philosophies and principles. Pay philosophies include market competitiveness (target total compensation levels vis-à-vis the market), pay for performance (level of differentiation between top and bottom performers) and quota participation rate (percent of participants achieving quota). Principles include topics such as strategy/job alignment, pay for performance, motivational and simple. As companies scale and mature, it becomes increasingly important to communicate how their philosophies and principles translate into specific plan design standards in the form of component guidelines. Component guidelines include eligibility, target total compensation, pay mix, leverage/upside, performance measures, mechanics, quotas/goals and special incentives/rewards.

GOALPOSTS: NONE → GOALPOSTS

Policy goalposts define acceptable ranges for each plan component. Simply stated, goalposts are the application of component guidelines to each specific platform job. Small and scaling companies typically don't require goalposts. However, large companies with multiple business units need them. Goalposts allow business units the flexibility to develop their own plans while adhering to best-in-class and market competitive standards. They also provide a methodology for evaluating plan designs across business units for the same platform job.

PROCESS: CALENDAR → WORK PLAN → PROCESS MAP WITH USER GUIDES

Small companies generally don't need a high-level calendar articulating key work streams and due dates. Activity ownership is simple. Only a few people are involved in managing the plans. As the number of jobs and people grows, companies need to articulate clearly, who is doing what and when to prevent duplication and gaps within the process. Scaling companies need a detailed work plan that articulates all the activities, owners and dates for each of the end-to-end process phases (plan, design, implement, administer, assess and manage). Mature companies with multiple business units developing plans need even more structure. They require a detailed process map and user guides (focused on key process steps such as assessments, costing and communications) to ensure they thoroughly train all business unit resources on how to effectively do their jobs.

GOVERNANCE: FUNCTIONAL OWNERSHIP → R&R → RACI'S AND MULTILEVEL COMMITTEES

Startup companies typically have a small team of key stakeholders responsible for the sales compensation program. All they need is a simple list of responsibilities by function (e.g., sales, sales operations, finance, HR). As they grow, it becomes necessary to detail out the roles and responsibilities for each job within a function (e.g., HR compensation versus the HR business partner). Scaling companies should also structure a sales compensation committee that resolves escalations and exceptions throughout the year. Mature companies should conduct a RACI (Responsible, Accountable, Consulted and Informed) analysis across their process map to clearly articulate responsibilities throughout the end-to-end process. They should also consider a multilevel sales compensation committee to accommodate the multiple business units.

Do you have the right foundational sales compensation program management practices in place for your company's growth stage?

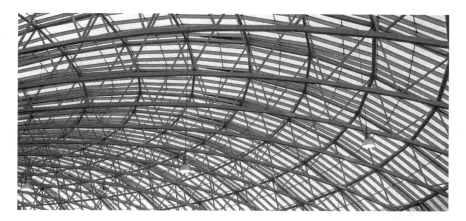

Effective Sales Compensation Design: Using Sales Compensation Principles

As the new fiscal year approaches, companies prepare for the annual process of updating the sales compensation program. Those in charge of driving the process often "gear up" knowing in advance how lengthy the discussions can be, driven by earnest opinions and evolving business objectives. To accelerate the annual design process, we recommend a process that defines a corporate-wide set of principles to govern sales compensation design and execution. We call this a "Principle Driven Sales Compensation Framework" (see the following example). The framework includes a goal, guiding principles, component guidelines and foundational guidelines. The framework does not specify a specific in-year plan design. Instead, it provides market-competitive and philosophy-aligned design guidelines within which all plans must live. The key to a successful framework is that it stays stable over time. As such, it reflects a true long-term company philosophy not influenced by fiscal year goals and objectives.

Develop Governing Rules Using Best-in-Class Framework

GOAL ▸	Attract, Retain and Reward Best-in-Class Sales Talent to Profitably Grow the Business									
GUIDING PRINCIPLES ▸	Aligned to Strategy and Job			Motivational and Market Competitive			Pay for Persuasion and Performance		Consistent, Transparent and Simple	
COMPONENT GUIDELINES ▸	Eligibility	Pay Levels	Pay Mix	Leverage (Upside)	Measures and Weights	Mechanics and Pay Curve	Performance and Payout Periods	Quotas/ Targets	Crediting and Policies	Special Incentives
FOUNDATIONAL GUIDELINES ▸	Investment/ROI		Communication		Administration			Process and Governance		

Before building a principle framework, companies must spend time with the C-suite to confirm its reward philosophies with regard to key areas such as:

- The role of sales compensation as a lever for performance management

- Total pay relative to competitors for talent and level of differentiation in pay between high and low performers

- Expected level of quota participation (i.e., the percent of the population achieving quota)

- Levels of consistency versus variance across various regions or business units

Designers work with their C-suite to develop a set of guiding principles to support their philosophies (see second row in framework example). Principles are a set of guiding rules that govern the overall program design.

The next level of the framework articulates the company's guidance for all the components of a plan design—from guidelines on what makes a role eligible for a sales plan through proper use of add-on bonuses such as spiffs or contests (see the 10 component areas detailed in the framework example). A task force should convene to spell out these guidelines and ensure that they reinforce the guiding principles.

Lastly, the framework also includes a section of foundational guidelines, which provide standards for how the company will manage the sales compensation program. Herein, the framework lays out guidance on how the company will cost, communicate, administer and govern the program.

While it takes effort to build out and obtain executive sign-off, the framework offers tremendous value to the company. Most importantly, a principle-driven approach virtually assures that companies incorporate industry best practices into the design of sales compensation plans. Secondly, having a framework to fall back on will alleviate the rat holes that plan design committees often run into with the many plan design requests. This results in time that can be better used to discuss sales strategy and how the sales compensation plan can support that effort.

Sales compensation leaders may also leverage the principle framework to educate leadership and other key stakeholders involved in the design process. A by-product of providing education is that sales compensation leaders elevate the perception of their role as strategic advisors as opposed to tactical facilitators. This is especially true when they are able to provide both the principles framework and the reasoning behind each guideline.

Summing it all up, a "Principle Driven Sales Compensation Framework" delivers lots of value to the sales compensation leader. Instead of "gearing up," sales compensation professionals can focus on delivering strategic value and staying ahead of the game.

Platform Jobs: The Secret to Manage Sales Comp in Big Companies

Managing the sales compensation program for a large company with hundreds of titles and thousands of salespeople, spanning across the globe deploying dozens and dozens of different customer contact roles can be a challenge. What's the best way to drive consistency and avoid being bogged down in complexity, turf battles and corporate bureaucracy? It's not enough to have best plan design "know-how." Sales compensation stakeholders need a disciplined process to guide the organization to success.

Here are the three tenants of our sales compensation program management framework.

1. **Platform Jobs.** Platform jobs are groupings of titles performing similar duties based on specific attributes into common job types.

2. **Sales Compensation Principles and Goalposts.** Principles are a set of governing rules and best practices to steer compensation design decisions and program governance. Goalposts are a set of

values or ranges for each compensation plan component based on best practices and company needs.

3. **Sales Compensation Governance.** Governance describes the internal process, roles and responsibilities and timing for end-to-end management of sales compensation.

PLATFORM JOBS: A CLOSER LOOK

Let's dive into the details on platform jobs, including what they are, how to develop them and how to maximize their benefits.

WHAT ARE PLATFORM JOBS?

Platform jobs are groupings of titles performing similar duties based on specific attributes into common job types.
Examples of specific attribute types:

- Customer focus: direct, partner, technical

- Expertise: generalist, specialist

- Segment: global, large, medium, small

- Route to market: direct, indirect, both

- Sales strategy: convert new customers, retain existing customers, penetrate existing customers

- Sales process: assess, persuade, fulfill, renew, optimize

- Deployment: accounts, narrow geography, wide geography

- Management responsibility: individual contributor, team leader, manager

Companies should customize the list of attributes based on business type and coverage needs. For example, a direct-only sales force may not require "route-to-market" attributes.

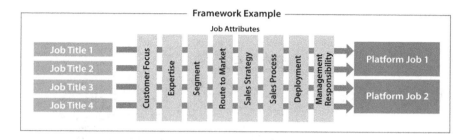

The following is an example of a territory sales rep platform job. The client had multiple job titles across its BUs and segments, which were essentially playing the same role; yet, plan designs varied significantly across these roles. However, in all cases, the territory sales rep focused on retaining and growing existing customers and acquiring new customers within an assigned geographic territory. This is a good example of the value of creating platform jobs.

Build a decision tree to articulate each unique platform job (see the following example). Decision trees are great tools for articulating the decision criteria for each platform job. If sales managers want to add a new job to the organization, they can select the best job using the decision trees.

PLATFORM JOB DECISION TREE EXAMPLE

The number of platform jobs depends on the range of business models, routes to market and sales motions. Most large sales entities will have less than 50 platform jobs, but some of the largest sales forces have up to 100 platform jobs. This may sound like a lot, but it's not really, when compared to 1,000-plus different job titles.

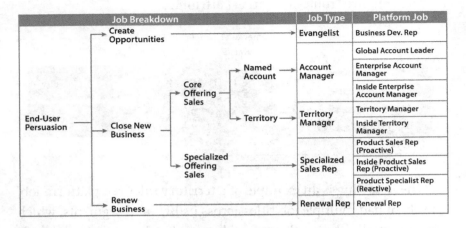

Job Breakdown			Job Type	Platform Job
End-User Persuasion	Create Opportunities		Evangelist	Business Dev. Rep
	Close New Business	Core Offering Sales → Named Account	Account Manager	Global Account Leader
				Enterprise Account Manager
				Inside Enterprise Account Manager
		Core Offering Sales → Territory	Territory Manager	Territory Manager
				Inside Territory Manager
		Specialized Offering Sales	Specialized Sales Rep	Product Sales Rep (Proactive)
				Inside Product Sales Rep (Proactive)
				Product Specialist Rep (Reactive)
	Renew Business		Renewal Rep	Renewal Rep

HOW TO DEVELOP PLATFORM JOBS

Developing a set of platform jobs is an involved task. It involves fact-finding, documentation, task force meetings, decision-making, mapping and implementation planning.

KEY STEPS

1. **Collect, Document and Confirm Current Jobs and Their Attributes.**
   - Gather all go-to-market, sales and HR job titles/descriptions, organization charts and deployment data.
   - Create a job profile template (PowerPoint and/or Excel) with all relevant attributes.
   - Interview and/or work with HR, sales ops and sales management to complete job profile templates.
   - Split out job titles if multiple roles exist under that title.
   - Confirm local variations and needs (e.g., hybrid jobs in emerging countries).

2. **Determine Key Attributes to Classify Jobs.**
   - Determine key attributes to create the level one job classification.

- Options include:
  - > Job families (e.g., direct field, direct inside, specialist, technical, channel, renewals).
  - > Persuasion points (end-user, partner, technical).
- Socialize and confirm job classification with HR and sales ops.

3. **Develop Platform Jobs and Decision Tree.**
   - Review attributes for all jobs within each job classification to consolidate similar jobs into an initial set of platform jobs.
   - Use additional attributes to build out a decision tree within each job classification that clearly results in a relevant platform job.
   - Update platform jobs based on the decision tree design.
   - Use the decision tree for communication and ongoing management.

4. **Map Current Jobs to Confirm Structure and Create Platform Job Profiles.**
   - Map all current titles (HR titles, business titles, comp titles, etc.) to new platform jobs and identify gaps.
   - Work with HR, sales ops and sales comp to confirm structure.
   - Update/finalize platform jobs and the decision tree based on mapping and feedback.
   - Create platform job profiles to summarize each unique job.

5. **Slot Incumbents to New Titles and Implement Changes.**
   - Develop employee-slotting worksheet and complete first-pass slotting based on title mapping.
   - Work with HR and sales ops to complete slotting.
   - Develop transition strategy, communication work plan and materials.
   - Obtain approval from sales leadership.
   - Complete communications rollout.

Building and managing a codified set of platform jobs has many sales coverage and sales compensation management benefits.

Sales Coverage Management. Platform jobs are an effective framework to design, operationalize and assess job roles and productivity.

- Align consistently to business needs and strategy across BUs, regions, segments, verticals.

- Use common language and framework to drive operational efficiencies for planning, deployment, enablement, reporting and sales comp.

- Provide a framework to appropriately analyze and compare sales force metrics (e.g., sales cost analysis, headcount ratios, span of control) to drive accountability and productivity.

- Evaluate how many resources actually reside in each platform role to better manage coverage and COS objectives.

Sales Compensation Management. Platform jobs are an effective framework to design, manage and assess sales compensation pay levels and plans.

- Inform job mapping with third-party survey sources to improve pay level benchmarking.

- Utilize best-in-class plan design goalposts (guidelines for pay mix, upside opportunity, measure types, performance period, etc.) to drive consistent and best practices.

- Assign incumbents within a platform job to the right plan to drive better alignment with the company's philosophies and market-best practices.

- Consolidate similar plans within the same platform job to reduce plan proliferation

- Provide a framework to appropriately analyze and compare pay and performance analytics, sales force survey results and plan assessments to improve plan design effectiveness. .

- Assess all plans against defined goalposts to ensure alignment with the company's philosophies and market-best practices.

CALL TO ACTION

Do you manage a large sales organization? If so, how do you manage your job titles? Do you have the right number of job titles? Does your company use multiple roles within a job title, multiple job titles for the same role or both? Are you having challenges comparing analytics across different sales organizations with similar jobs? Use platform job decision trees to address these issues.

Effective Governance: Making Sales Compensation Successful

Sales compensation needs a strong governance model. The lack of strong governance practices can result in some of the following symptoms:

1. Plans and quotas introduced well after the fiscal year has started

2. Excessive questions from the field inquiring about how the plan works

3. Frequent crediting and payment disputes with no defined resolution pathway

4. Regular finger-pointing between those responsible for program management

These symptoms are consistent with an absent governance model. Many sales organizations allocate substantial resources to plan design.

However, they fail to allocate the time and investment necessary to ensure the right systems, policies and processes are in place to make the sales compensation program operate smoothly.

A Complete Governance Framework. Effective governance models link together the five phases of the sales compensation program.

1. **Plan:** Capturing critical sales compensation design inputs such as sales strategy and business objectives, sales strategy and coverage model, and sales job roles and responsibilities.

2. **Design:** Working with multiple functional groups to develop plans that align to sales objectives and drive the right behaviors.

3. **Implement:** Setting up targets and territories, crediting rules and policies, and communicating plans to sales incumbents.

4. **Administer:** Calculating and processing payments, providing reports, managing exceptions and resolving disputes.

5. **Assess:** Analyzing plan effectiveness to identify future change requirements.

BUILDING THE SOLID GOVERNANCE MODEL

What is included in an effective governance model? The Alexander Group recommends putting the following four pieces in place.

1. **An End-to-End Process.** Build a comprehensive set of all the execution steps from the plan phase through the assess phase. This may sound easy, but after engaging all of those involved with the sales

compensation program and mapping out the entire process, bigger companies may have more than 100 unique steps, each requiring time and resources to execute. However, once completed, you now have the foundation to execute, with clarity and transparency, all the steps of sales compensation program management. The following is an example of detailed mapping.

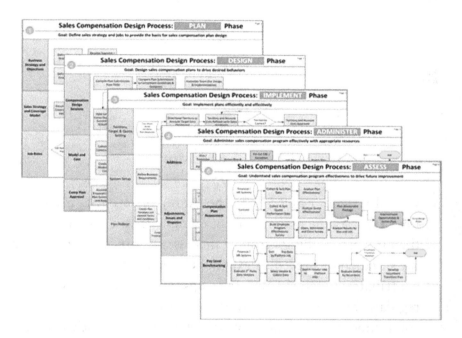

2. **Roles and Responsibilities.** The next logical activity is to document the assignment of owners, approvers and supporters by functional group for each step in the end-to-end process. It can sometimes be a challenge to agree on who should be doing what, because it requires people to commit to doing something that may not fall within their traditional job function. However, the benefits of having a well-thought-out accountability grid can be felt over the short term and long term. Within a specific plan cycle, all participants can be clearly aware of who is doing what so the process moves efficiently. A best-in-class accountability grid covers all program steps. See the following example.

Roles & Responsibilities — Administer Phase

Process Area	Process Step	Exec Ldrshp	Sales Ldrshp	Sales Mgmt.	Sales Ops	HR/ Comp	Finance	Accting/ Payroll	IT	Legal
Payment Processing	Generate Commissions Statements									
	Commissions Statements									
	Send Statements to Incumbents									
Participant Additions	Hire/Transition New Participants (sub-process)									
	Assign Plan & Territory									
	Fill Out Handling Forms									
	Load into System									
	Review Plans (Reps & Mgrs)									
	Sign Off? *(skip next step if yes)*									
	Determine Root Cause & Fix									

Key: Step   Decision   Document   Owner   Supporter   Approver

3. **Global Calendar and SLAs.** The timing of activities is equally important as the assignment of owners. If you miss this step, then the probability of trouble increases significantly. Consider the situation of a recent Alexander Group client whose program contributors—across sales, sales ops, HR, finance, legal, etc.— regularly bickered because functional groups didn't have shared commitment on the timing of key deliverables. The bickering created distrust, indifference and a delayed domino effect, ultimately, leading to the introduction of plans halfway through the year.

An effective global calendar includes all the end-to-end process steps sequenced in the right order with specific start and completion times. Many steps within the sales compensation management program rely on outputs from preceding steps. Clear ownership and deadlines within necessary time frames help ensure key dependencies associated with each step are handled in an effective manner.

4. **Sales Compensation Committees and Escalation Pathways.** The last critical piece is forming a sales compensation governance

committee, which meets regularly to address issues such as rep performance, plan effectiveness, plan cost actuals versus accruals, management exceptions and crediting disputes. Large organizations tend to rely on a multilevel committee hierarchy to ensure minor issues are resolved at the local level while bringing in senior leadership to address larger issues that could not be resolved at lower levels. Best-in-class committees come in multiple shapes and sizes. Regardless of how they are structured, these committees share the following fundamental characteristics:

- A defined charter with representation from multiple functional groups
- Clear escalation pathways that define the what, when, who and how of issue escalation
- A repository for plan improvement suggestions

A fully functional governance committee creates confidence in the sales compensation program, because participants know their concerns will be addressed and ideas will be considered for next year's plan design.

An effective governance model is a prerequisite to effectively scaling a company's sales compensation program. Building the right infrastructure, including process maps, roles and responsibilities, global calendars and governance committees, can save a lot of time and ensure the sales compensation program continues to run smoothly.

Create Design Goalposts to Manage Sales Compensation Plan Consistency

Salespeople in the same role should all be on the same sales compensation plan. Right? You may be surprised to hear that many companies, particularly ones with large sales forces spanning the globe, struggle to manage the desired level of consistency in plan designs for the same role across the company.

A Widespread Problem. Consider a recent example where the sales compensation executive was analyzing sales compensation plans for the company's primary selling role, the territory sales representative. Here are the findings.

- Pay mix ranged from 40/60 to 70/30.

- Some territory sales reps had one bookings measure while others had five separate management by objectives (MBOs).

- Territory sales reps in Europe had 2x accelerators and capped plans while reps in the U.S. had 3x accelerators and no caps.

Sales leaders and HR executives regularly find themselves in this situation as the result of a decentralized plan design process. Region leaders have autonomy to make decisions often with limited governance and oversight from headquarters. The end result: Not all plans align to the desired behaviors of the job, incumbents in the same sales job have unequal earnings potential and measuring plan effectiveness for that job just got a lot harder.

Plan Design Goalposts. Companies with best-in-class sales compensation programs avoid this situation by establishing a concrete set of goalposts to guide the development of sales compensation plans globally. The definition of goalposts is simple: a set of design parameters for all components of a company's sales incentive plan. For plans to receive approval, the designs must pass through goalposts for each element ranging from pay mix to crediting rules. While the definition is simple, the creation of goalposts is not. Many stakeholders, whether they reside in HR, sales, finance or operations, often have different opinions about what the ideal sales compensation plan should look like. Sometimes these opinions, which also include beliefs and philosophies, are difficult to reconcile. Consider how commonly finance and sales argue over commission accelerators! Finance wants to manage costs while sales wants to maximize rewards for over-performers. Yet, more importantly, even within the sales organization, there is often disagreement among different sales leaders based upon their histories, experiences and varying philosophies on sales compensation design.

Plan design goalposts are a great way to get your company's sales compensation program under control. There are many benefits of plan design goalposts:

- Sales job and sales compensation plan alignment 95% of the time or higher

- Increased plan consistency and fewer plan exceptions

- Saved time and manpower through a faster and more efficient incentive design process

- Balance between centralized control and local need flexibility

- Greater ability to evaluate plan effectiveness by role

Getting Started. To best start the journey, it pays to be prepared. Have a clear plan and process that involves the right stakeholders so you can avoid (or at least minimize) the amount of conflict and headaches along the way.

Step No. 1: Design Goalposts. Make sure to involve sales, finance, operations, HR groups and other key stakeholders. Get people in a room and hash things out. Involve representatives from different regions to see where local market practices require unique treatment. Having a consistent set of sales platform jobs will significantly simplify this process, preventing confusion between job titles and the work people are actually performing. If platform jobs are out of date or do not exist, do this work first. Next, as a team, work through the sales compensation goalpost decisions by job family, and secure agreement on appropriate sales compensation goalposts for each job. Keep iterating goalpost design until the team reaches executive level agreement. The end-result should look something like Figure 1.

Pay Mix	Pay Mix Range: 50/50 to 60/40			Draw eligible: Yes	
Leverage	Leverage: 3x				
Measures	# of Measures: 1–2	Measure Type: Bookings Margin Revenue MBO	Level: Territory Individual	Weight Range: 80% 20%	
MBOs	MBO Eligible: Yes # of MBO Components: 2 max MBO Component Options:		Pipeline Development ☒	Partner Development ☐	Product Objectives ☒
Mechanics & Pay Curve	Formula Type: Individual Commission Rate ☐ Commission ☐ Bonus Formula ☒ Add-on Bonus ☐		Mechanics Eligibility: Thresholds Caps Decelerator	Yes ☐ ☐ ☒	No ☒ ☒ ☐
Performance & Payout Periods	Performance Periods Quota-Based Measures: Annually MBO-Based Measures: Quarterly		Payout Periods Quota-Based Measures: Monthly MBO-Based Measures: Quarterly		

Figure 1: Example Goalpost Composite

Step No. 2: Conduct a Goalpost Alignment Test. This step involves evaluating current incumbent plans against the newly designed goalposts. Collect sales compensation plan designs for all titles within a platform job. The information should include target pay mix, measures, mechanics and any other pertinent plan design components. Next, match every title and plan incumbent to the appropriate platform job and compare the actual plan designs to the platform job goalposts to determine the gaps. Gather all the incumbent data for each plan within each platform job. Compile the individual gaps into cumulative results. Don't be surprised to see some big numbers! Gap tests regularly show hundreds of incumbents and/or millions of target incentive dollars outside established goalposts.

$11.3M   **Pay Mix:** Amount of misaligned target incentive due to pay mix being too conservative or aggressive
➡ *Pay mix out of sync with level of sales influence — % of pay at risk should be commensurate with a job's impact on the sales process*

$8.2M   **Leverage:** Amount associated with gap between actual leverage payouts vs. goalpost leverage
➡ *Misaligned upside earnings distort relationship between top-performer pay and selling difficulty, sales influence and quota size*
➡ *Uneven upside opportunity within a platform job can impact morale, motivation and attrition over time*

$10.8M   **Plan Period:** Amount of misaligned target incentive due to some reps being on quarterly rather than annual plans
➡ *Plan periods out of sync with sales cycle length and strategic-selling focus*
➡ *Excessive sales ops time spent building and publishing quotas takes time away from other productivity and enablement activities*

Figure 2: Example Goalpost Analysis

Step No. 3: Update Plans to Align With Goalposts. This step requires executive approval to overhaul the misaligned plans. Incentive misalignment exists at most companies, but the magnitude of the problem varies and often hides from management. Associating numbers with the problem (as shown in Figure 2) is a great way to get management's attention. Millions of incentive dollars may be at risk and desired selling behaviors could be compromised by earning potential inequality and dilution of focus. Gaps like these can ultimately lead to ineffective performance, misspent sales compensation dollars and attrition.

Step No. 4: Transition to New Plans. The final step requires careful transition planning to implement new plans compliant with your goalposts. While the short-term transition process may be difficult, the long-term benefits are compelling. With good goalposts in place, you now have a menu of plan options and mandates that can direct incentive design decisions for several years to come, saving lots of time and energy, not to mention fewer disputes and change requests landing on your desk.

Sales Compensation Goalposts—
Global Solution Case Study

Global companies seeking to design effective sales compensation plans on a worldwide basis should employ platform jobs and design goalposts to reduce complexity and design cycle times.

Platform jobs group sales roles together for similar but not identical job titles. Within each platform role, multiple use cases may exist reflecting unique strategic focus for the individual job. Goalposts provide the range of sanctioned sales compensation design choices available to local sales entities.

Let's examine a client's need to create sales compensation goalposts for 20-plus platform jobs across three geographic regions. In this case example, first-line managers could select the preferred sales compensation plan for their sales roles. Unfortunately, this client experienced an exceptionally long annual planning process and managers often selected plans, which did not fit with the organization's vision for the job roles. The variations centered on local choice regarding level and weightings of plan measures. The back and forth between HQ and local management was tedious and time-consuming and not always producing the optimal outcome.

The Alexander Group helped design and implement a process, which would result in greater global plan consistency as well as fewer cycles spent on the plan assignment process. After a set of initial planning meetings, the team determined the best course of action was to provide first-line managers with a packet of plan options as determined by a role's particular use cases. Additionally HQ would provide guidance and training on when to select which plan option.

These steps developed a process for providing better HQ direction to local design efforts.

Step No. 1: Identify Job Roles. The first step focused on the company's existing plans, which had variations in each role. The team conducted interviews with sales management in all geographic areas to understand how local management deployed each job. Differences in customer and product focus quickly emerged. Individuals in the same role may focus on one division in a single account or a broad swath of smaller accounts; they might sell the entire portfolio or a single product line. We cataloged these differences, as well as goal assignment methods, into specific use cases.

Step No. 2: Assign Measure Levels and Weighting to Each Use Case. Secondly, the team created a set of plan options for each role. These options aligned to specific use cases. The team featured these options in the training program for first-line managers, who continue to have responsibility for selecting plans for their direct reports. A committee of sales management from each geography, as well as operations and compensation center of excellence representatives, gathered to vet each defined use case and assign plan measure guidance. After a number of iterations, the team approved final goalposts and guidelines and they were ready for delivery to field management.

Develop detailed measure and weight guidelines for each platform job's measure goalpost based on deployment/focus to drive consistent strategies.

────────── Framework Example ──────────

| Platform Job | Measure Goalpost | Measure/Weight Guidelines (Reviewed Annually) |

JOB	ROLE	MEASURE CATEGORY & WEIGHTS	DEPLOYMENT/FOCUS	SALES MEASURES & WEIGHTS GUIDELINES
Account Manager	Associate Account Manager	100% Sales	Territory	70% Total/30% Team Total
			Product/Service	80% Product/20% Service
	Account Manager	100% Sales	Territory	70% Total/30% Team Total
			Product/Service	80% Product/20% Service
			Account	80% Total/20% Service
			Architecture	80% Product Set/20% Service
			Channel	80% Total/20% MS
			No Meaningful Service Goal	100% Total
	Global Account Manager/ Strategic Account Manager	80% Sales + 20% KSO	Territory	75% Total/25% Team Total
			Product/Service	75% Product/25% Service
			Account	75% Total/25% Service
			No Meaningful Service Goal	100% Total

Figure 1: Goalposts—Measure/Weight Guidelines

Step No. 3: Design an Exception Request Process. The final step was to create a process to address exceptions. The designed guidelines were appropriate in most cases, but given the global nature of the organization, exception requests did arise. Considerations were made for defined conditions, which were vetted by internal team leadership before moving to the global compensation center of excellence for final approval. If the requests did not meet requirements for a unique plan, management received guidance in selecting a suitable plan from the established list.

The creation of these guidelines, as well as the robust involvement of stakeholders from across the organization–field, operations, global compensation center of excellence–drove significant adoption. During the plan's first year in use, exception requests were about 30% fewer than the previous year. In addition, the sales compensation planning process was tracking on time, a significant improvement. Utilizing use-case specific plan guidelines, along with clear explanations why, greatly decreased friction in the plan assignment process, driving consistency across global organizations and freeing-up valuable time for both sales and operations functions.

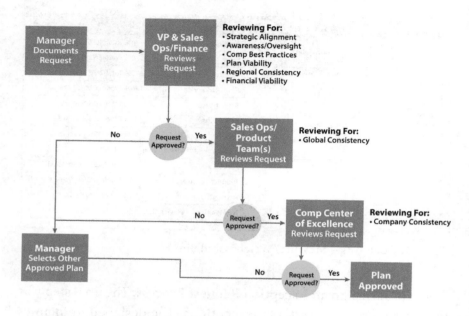

Figure 2: Plan Exception Request Process

Sales Quota Perspectives

Articles in Section

◆

Building Your Sales Quota Program

5 Best Sales Quotas Practices

Setting Sales Quotas: 3 Tricky Rep Types to Tackle

11th-Hour Quotas: Last-Minute Checks to Finalize
Next Year's Assignments

Sales Quotas: How to Select the Right Allocation Methodology

How to Analyze Your Quota Distributions

Get Confident About Setting New Product Quotas:
5 Things to Consider

Building Your Sales Quota Program

Building a sound quota program is an important part of the annual sales planning cycle. Most sales leaders aim for 55% to 60% of their reps to achieve or exceed quota. Unfortunately, few sales leaders devote enough time to build and maintain a systematic quota program that effectively supports achieving results on a consistent basis.

Setting correct quotas does not need to be bureaucratic or complex. Know and apply the five key elements to doing it right.

No. 1: Quota Methodology. Effective quota programs begin with a sound methodology. There are many factors to consider, including type and quantity of accounts, historical performance, territory potential, funnel potential, competitor threats, market share and other factors. Here are five quota-setting methodologies:

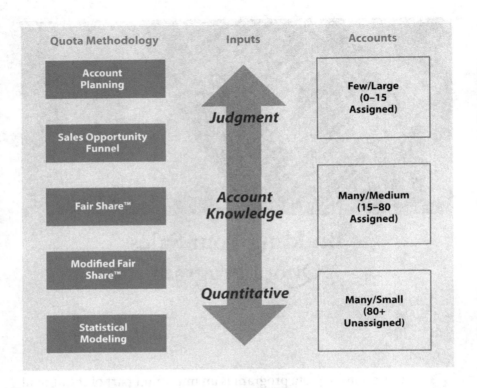

Quota Methodology	Inputs	Accounts
Account Planning	Judgment	Few/Large (0–15 Assigned)
Sales Opportunity Funnel		
Fair Share™	Account Knowledge	Many/Medium (15–80 Assigned)
Modified Fair Share™	Quantitative	Many/Small (80+ Unassigned)
Statistical Modeling		

No. 2: Allocation Process. The quota allocation process is the disbursement of the annual sales objective. It is who, what and when of quotas. The challenge of quota allocation lies in the need for cross-functional involvement. Sales leadership, sales ops, field sales, finance and HR all need to be involved in some capacity. Cross-functionality also helps inform auxiliary issues related to quotas such as alignment to new compensation measures, account transfers, ramps for new hires, terminations and other issues.

No. 3: Accountability. Who should own the process? Sales management owns and leads it. The process begins when finance gives them the final goals before they kick off the process. Often, sales leaders wait until finance delivers the target number. However, the sales leader shouldn't wait for this to get the process started. Sales leaders can begin building goals based on a bottom-up approach. This way when the top-down numbers are ready, the sales leaders can quickly and confidently reconcile the numbers and allocate quotas for the coming year.

No. 4: Communication. Sales leadership communicates quotas to their team. Communicate at the same time any other changes such as changes to roles, territories and compensation plans. Get these communicated soon after the start of the fiscal year. Being late is problematic. Leaders can avoid this with a sound sales quota program, which includes a well-thought-out methodology, process and timeline.

No. 5: Audit. Track attainments and analyze drivers of distributions during the year. You will be well-informed to make adjustments to the methodology and to the overall quota program, too. However, try to avoid making mid-year quotas changes. Most companies (72% of the respondents from a previous *Sales Compensation Trends Survey*) change fewer than 10% of incumbent quotas mid-year. Changing more than 10% of incumbent quotas likely reflects a quota program that is functioning poorly. If you're in this group, you may need an urgent and complete overhaul of your program.

Building a sound quota program does not have to be complicated. It does need to include the above elements for broad confidence across the company. How your individual sales reps "climb their hills" is important. Knowing that they can achieve their goals and earn their sales compensation depends on an effective quota program.

5 Best Sales Quotas Practices

Sales quotas are a popular but imperfect sales management tool. Each year, sales leadership allocates the company's annual forecast to the sales team. The process is loaded with noise, challenge and drama. Logically, it seems that these annual attempts to get quotas right would eventually yield a highly tuned system, celebrated by all. Unfortunately, this is not the case. In a recent survey, more than 60% of the participating companies reported, "correct goal/quota setting" as the No. 1 challenge facing the sales compensation program.

The sales quota program is a performance accountability system. These systems can create, at times, a tense, charged environment. Because setting quotas is both science and art, it is open to errors and criticisms from all fronts.

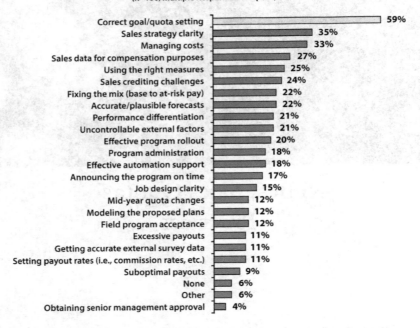

Sales Compensation Challenges
(n=100, Multiple Responses Accepted)

Correct goal/quota setting	59%
Sales strategy clarity	35%
Managing costs	33%
Sales data for compensation purposes	27%
Using the right measures	25%
Sales crediting challenges	24%
Fixing the mix (base to at-risk pay)	22%
Accurate/plausible forecasts	22%
Performance differentiation	21%
Uncontrollable external factors	21%
Effective program rollout	20%
Program administration	18%
Effective automation support	18%
Announcing the program on time	17%
Job design clarity	15%
Mid-year quota changes	12%
Modeling the proposed plans	12%
Field program acceptance	12%
Excessive payouts	11%
Getting accurate external survey data	11%
Setting payout rates (i.e., commission rates, etc.)	11%
Suboptimal payouts	9%
None	6%
Other	6%
Obtaining senior management approval	4%

Follow these five best practices to improve your sales quota program.

No. 1: Embrace Sales Quotas. Yes, sales quotas drive performance accountability (and produce noise). More importantly, they offer a broad and robust sales management platform for sales planning conversations and coaching. Sales quota allocation provides an excellent process to judge current sales results and assess future sales opportunities. In many respects, it is one of sales management's most important planning and management tools. Use quota results to recognize success and identify performance improvement opportunities.

No. 2: Let Customer Knowledge Drive Allocation Process. Should sales personnel be involved in setting their own quotas? Conventional wisdom encourages seller involvement in the annual quota allocation process. When sales management involves sales personnel in the process, they engage and commit more to achieving their sales objectives. Yes, there is a wide arc of selling. For example, some sellers have only one account, such as strategic account managers (SAMs). These sellers work year-round with the same buyers at the assigned customer, often working on large complex deals featuring high-revenue opportunities. Of course, we would want the SAMs to be deeply involved in the quota allocation process. Who else knows more about the account—its revenue potential—than the SAM assigned to the account? Meanwhile, an inbound sales associate taking calls driven by marketing campaigns has little personal knowledge of sales potential. It is best to use information about marketing campaigns, their duration, offer and historical impact to help set quotas for telesales associates. Extent of customer knowledge determines the appropriate involvement of sales personnel. The more they know about the accounts, the more involved they are in the process. The less they know about the accounts, the less they participate in suggesting the right quota.

No. 3: Use Potential to Fine-Tune Quotas. Between the two selling extremes of strategic account managers and telesales associates exists many types of sellers; the most common is the account manager. Account managers have a specific set of accounts, often called "named" accounts. Some of these accounts are very active and well known to the account manager, others less so. We would like our account managers actively involved in the quota allocation process. We want them to understand both their active and inactive accounts. Additionally, sales management can employ strong account-by-account analytics to create predictive potential estimates for accounts. Combining the account manager's view of next year's potential with the calculated estimates by sales management offers a dialog opportunity known as the "top-down/bottom-up" quota allocation process where both parties contribute to establishing the annual quota. This methodology trumps quota allocation processes that take last year's performance and add a flat growth rate.

No. 4: Make Quotas Active. Quota performance, quota reporting and quota reviews should be in the lifeblood of sales management narrative and operations. Leadership's messaging to the sales force should ingrain quota performance. Remind the sales team—and often—of the shared quota commitments. Quota reporting should be available to all, including sales force-wide numbers down to individual performance. They should not be private—let them be transparent. Let them see how other sellers are doing and how they compare. Use quota performance to inform sales coaching and management efforts. Quotas should not reside solely on spreadsheets; make them an active part of the management process.

No. 5: Manage Crediting, Exceptions and Mid-Year Changes. Walk the quota ramparts to ensure the integrity of the program. Make sure the program does not offer excessive double crediting. Double crediting of 10% or less is a good starting benchmark to assess the extent of double crediting. To calculate double crediting, take compensable revenue less actual revenue divided by actual revenue. Limit mid-year exceptions. Publish definitive and restrictive rules when sales management can provide "quota relief." Use a quota review board to approve all quota adjustments. Only consider sales force-wide mid-year changes when the company has restated it goals and publishes those new goals to the stockholders/owners.

KNOWN SALES QUOTA TRAPS

Here are two common sales quota "traps" that sales leaders can avoid. First, do not attempt to assign quotas for unpredictable, large orders. These orders can upend a quota system. Pay them on a separate schedule. Second, keep new products out of the annual quota, unless product management has a proven track record of hitting launch dates and accurately estimating volume. Otherwise, leave them out of the quota. Reward them with a spiff.

Quotas are more often right than wrong; however, the accompanying noise factor disproportionately distracts from the overall confidence of the allocated quotas. In other words, your quotas may not be that bad after all. Follow the five suggestions: Embrace sales quotas; let customer knowledge drive the allocation process; use potential to fine-tune quotas; make quotas active; and manage crediting, exceptions and mid-year changes. Of course, avoid the sales quota traps of mega orders and new products.

Setting Sales Quotas:
3 Tricky Rep Types to Tackle

Sales success begins with setting the right goals. Unfortunately, this is an area of chronic pain for sales reps and leaders. Most leaders are not confident they will hit their plan. In fact, more than 50% of sales reps miss their plan. According to the research in a recent edition of our annual *Sales Compensation Practices Survey*, less than 15% of sales leaders are highly confident in their team's ability to hit sales projections, and less than 50% of sales reps hit or exceeded their goals.

What is at the root of this challenge, and what can you do about it? Our research and experience suggests when it comes to setting quotas, there are a few specific rep populations, which require particular attention. Despite good intentions, the process sometimes "goes bad" for these populations of sellers. A quick program audit can determine if this is true for your sales force. The three groups in particular to watch for are:

- New sellers

- New Product sellers

- "Big-number" reps

1. **New Sellers.** Tenure typically plays a role in a sales rep's ability to sell and meet targets. Experience and exposure to products, services and sales process breeds success. It's the company's job, however, to set targets fairly—stretch but achievable—for its total seller population, regardless of tenure. Often, new sellers, who are "earning their stripes," systematically underperform (as a percent of goal) as compared to their seasoned veteran counterparts. In such cases, your quota program may be artificially creating winners and losers.

   A common way to effectively develop and motivate new sellers is to give them a ramping quota. The duration of the ramp will depend on the length of the sales cycle and the complexity of the sales. Typical ramp time is between six and twelve months but should be no longer than 18 months.

2. **New Product Sellers.** Setting goals for new products or new markets is inherently challenging. With little to no historical data and often, limited, market intelligence, it can seem like a guessing game. Guess too high and reps lose. Morale suffers and good reps leave. Guess too low and you risk blowing out quotas. The following graphs tell a common story of consistently high quota achievement in a core market (in this case, North America) and consistently poor attainment in a new market (EMEA).

   To limit the negative impact of guessing too low or too high, apply a few of the following tactics. (1) Set longer pay and performance periods (e.g., annual versus quarterly targets) to smooth out any short-term fluctuations in performance. (2) Set quotas at a level where sales revenue brought in by the sales rep covers the cost of the sales rep, i.e., cost-based quotas. (3) Provide sales reps with a commission rate (instead of guessing at a target) for each incremental sale. You may have to limit or even eliminate accelerated rates above quota. All three tactics limit your exposure to risk associated with uncertainty.

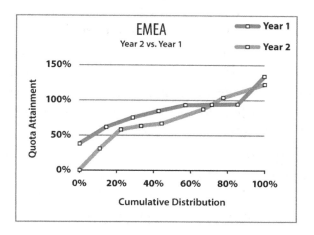

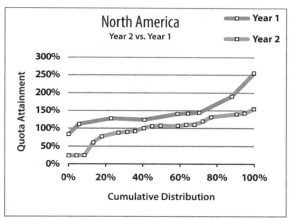

FIGURE 1. Systematically below-target performance in EMEA compared to North America across two years of data. All individuals below the 100% line have not met quota.

3. **"Big-Number" Reps.** The law of large numbers means it's hard to significantly exceed a big quota compared to a small quota. Consider the effort required to grow a $5 million territory by 10% versus a $50 million territory by 10%. If your organization applies a one-size-fits-all approach to annual quota increases (e.g.,

apply a flat percent growth over last year's results), you may be systematically creating winners and losers through your quota program. Your most seasoned reps with the biggest quotas may suffer the most. Recognize the difficulty in overachieving on a larger number, and set quotas for these reps based on an account planning and bottom-up goal setting approach as mentioned earlier. Discuss key inputs to next year's quotas with the sales reps, including expected customer churn and renewal rates, big deals in the pipeline, competitive displacement opportunities and general health of their territory. These discussions with each of your "big number" reps will allow you to have greater confidence in setting realistic targets for these reps. These discussions also go a long way in creating buy-in from the sales reps because they are actively involved in shaping their goals.

SAFEGUARDING AGAINST MISALLOCATION

Monitoring performance to identify these populations in your sales force is the first step toward isolating and solving the problem of misallocation. Simple measures like ramping goals for junior sales reps and detailed account planning with sellers managing few but large accounts will ensure the goals are as close to stretch but as achievable as possible. When setting targets or new product markets, keep it simple and consider cost-based quotas or flat commission rates. Finally, tailor your quota-setting process and allocation (e.g., top-down simple increase, bottom-up sales potential, account planning, fair/modified fair share, or a hybrid version of one of the above) based on account-level knowledge, historical data and management judgment.

11th-Hour Quotas:
Last-Minute Checks to Finalize
Next Year's Assignments

Quota allocation assigns the company's sales goal to sellers. The previous year's quota performance might not be exactly what was anticipated. The impending new fiscal year once again raises the same quota fairness challenges. Here are five items to help improve quota allocation confidence.

1. **Over-Allocation Check.** Over allocation of quota tends to drive skewed distributions. Approximately 50% of all companies over allocate quotas. The amount is typically between 5% and 10% of the corporate objective. Double check to ensure that over assignment is not excessive.

2. **Process Check.** You probably have a process for quotas outlining the "who, what and when" for setting, allocating and communicating the new quotas. Some companies have a sophisticated year-round process; others manage the process episodically.

Regardless of approach, there is always room for improvement. Now is the time, before you roll out the new quotas, to ensure that you've managed all of the steps correctly. Adding a process audit or a process check-in meeting is a good idea. This last minute opportunity may be the best time before year-end. It may also be a good time to document your process and guidelines properly, while the experience is still fresh in your mind.

3. **End-of-Year or Q4 Results.** Don't wait until the end of the year for the final numbers. Make assumptions the best you can. Determine probable Q4 and year-end performance. Too often, companies wait until all of the year-end results are complete before assigning quotas. This, by definition, will have you behind in the release of quotas for next year. Most of the time, these last-minute reconciliations don't change the big picture and materially impact next year's potential and performance goals. This may seem like a challenge if you have several big deals in the Q4 pipeline. However, don't underestimate the value of handing your sales reps their quotas at the start of the new year.

4. **Don't be Late.** Release the quotas as soon as possible. Late quotas can undermine leadership, showing that you are disorganized or maybe don't really understand the market potential or have clear objectives for next year.

5. **"Pre-Communicate" Quota Direction.** Sales leaders need to set fair individual quotas. They also need to build confidence in the sales rep's ability to achieve target. You can "pre-communicate" messages about the direction quotas are heading (e.g., up 10% to 15% from last year), and at the same time, communicate the key rationale for these changes (new product releases, new marketing campaigns, increased pricing, etc.). With salespeople (and most employees, for that matter), the less of a shock and surprise, the better.

Quota setting does not need to be bureaucratic or complex. Use simple but comprehensive methodologies. If necessary, late in the year, these last-minute checks can provide increased accuracy and supply the sales force with added confidence.

Sales Quotas: How to Select the Right Allocation Methodology

What is the right quota allocation method? Begin with a review of quota attainment from last year and this year. This is a smart first step and serves as a good baseline of how well the company or business unit allocates quotas, at least recently. Balanced and normal quota distributions likely require no change. However, if quota attainments are skewed or multimodal, perhaps it's time to select a new allocation methodology.

Start with Quota Process. It's the "who, what and when" of sales quotas. Sales and finance play a role. What about the actual sales representatives? Field sales involvement in the quota process is important, especially in cases where sales representatives have few accounts, and thus extensive knowledge about customer buying patterns. However, even as the number of accounts per salesperson increases and the knowledge of specific customers' decreases, the input of sales representatives is still quite useful. They provide quality forecast data. Participation in the process often boosts confidence in achieving quotas. Involving sales representatives also facilitates transparency, which can further reduce angst around how the "number" is calculated. However, Alexander Group surveys indicate only about one-third of its clients actually use sales representative-based inputs for sales quotas.

Select Allocation Methodology. Choose from among standard methodologies (see the following chart). Correlate the allocation methodology to one or more of the following: platform job type, number of assigned accounts, seller's knowledge of buyers, customer buying process or revenue segment. One quota methodology does not fit all. Typically, there would be at least two methodologies. The key is to match the number of methodologies to the number of prevalent sales motions deployed (see the following chart).

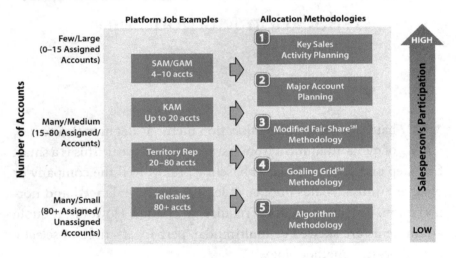

- **Account Managers (fewer than 15 accounts).** Strategic account manager (SAM) and similar account manager (AM) roles are usually hybrids of farming/hunting within large accounts and typically have long sales cycles. The good news: The longer sales cycle means these folks start the year with as much as six months of funnel opportunity. This is half of their annual quota—done. The bad news: They have to figure out the other portions of the quota. Even if everything goes according to plan, the timing of the closes (the long, lumpy sales cycles) can be erratic, causing booms and busts across quarters. This is typical. However, over the forecast period, experience shows that AMs sometime make overzealous bets on a handful of opportunities. This is challenging, resulting in bimodal clumping of winners and losers. Clear and consistent definition of funnel stages among AMs can smooth the distribution. Other consistent factors of account planning can help quota allocation, normalizing attainment results within this group. Utilize the first-line sales managers (FLSMs) here by allowing them full involvement; first-line involvement should be a natural extension of account planning. FLSMs should also be able to reign in and balance some of the AM bets for the coming year. Methodologies for this group include elements of account planning and funnel opportunities.

- **Territory Representatives (20–80 accounts).** Unlike the assigned handful of accounts of an AM, territory representatives have a longer list of prospects and thus need a different type of allocation methodology. However, in some cases, this group does have stratified target lists in which they can have a sub-group of high priority accounts—more of an AM-type motion. Be careful not to apply methodology only by sales role. For larger numbers of accounts, utilize historical data and broader modifiers such as the case with the Modified Fair Share^{SM} methodology. This methodology uses broader factors to modify historical territory results based on territory factors and on the individual representative's selling acumen.

Territory-Based Modifiers
- Market potential
- Market share
- Competitive threat
- Customer wallet share/product potential
- Historical sales in territory
- Current and historical funnel
- Time in territory

Individual Representative-Based Modifiers
- Tenure with firm
- Tenure in territory
- Tenure in position
- Sales experience
- Past performance/attainments

Of course, with a decent historical sample, the sales ops team can perform a regression analysis to determine the most relevant modifying factors (and weights) based on past results. While companies rarely do this, adoption of this methodology will allow you to make rational judgments, demonstrate competency and fairness to the territory representatives and build confidence.

- **Inside Sales (80-plus accounts).** For this highly transactional environment, an algorithm methodology is most appropriate. Typically, sellers know little about the individual buyers. Historical sample and macro-based modifiers (not modified locally at the territory level) such as firm pricing, global competition, market trends and GDP are examples of variables. Quota setting for this group of sellers usually reflects company shareholder growth percentage with little over allocation.

Get Help and Start Now. Don't procrastinate. It's understandable given the importance of hitting this year's number before worrying about setting next year's number. Taking the time to establish a sound plan and methodology pays big dividends. First map out the process, including how to involve seller input appropriately.

Next, choose the right allocation methodology. Successful sales leaders rely on their sales strategy, planning and operations teams to assist with data gathering, analysis and process management. Their support is critical as the larger sales organization focuses on this year's performance.

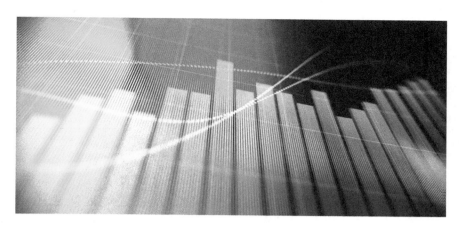

How to Analyze Your Quota
Distributions

The quota program is critical to driving top-line results and managing sales costs. Hidden in last period's performance data are insights about quota quality and effectiveness of the sales quota process. Every sales leader should have a routine process for analyzing quota distributions at a granular level (i.e., sub-groups such as geographies, job roles, tenure, products, accounts or industry verticals).

The Big Picture. Balanced quota distributions are critical to maintaining a well-motivated and cost-effective sales force. If not, undesirable results occur such as low morale, increased turnover, underpayments or overpayments of incentives. This results in a general failure to create the desired risk/reward environment. In any given period, typically about 60% of reps (and this can vary slightly by industry) should achieve hitting the plan or greater, and about 40% should be below goal.

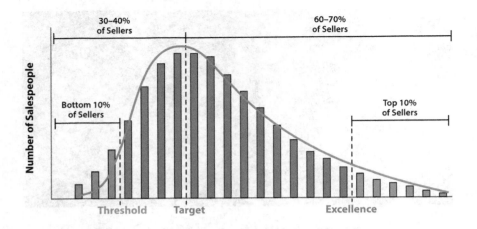

The Smaller (and More Interesting) Picture. Frequent review of attainment at the sub-group level ensures consistent quota management across the various subgroups, which helps to avoid potentially costly mistakes in quota misallocation. Here are three examples.

By Geography. This is a common and logical first cut. In general, expect similar results across geographies. Factors such as market maturity (e.g., developed versus emerging), economic growth or stability could impact quota distributions, particularly for a given period. However, sustained differences in quota distributions can be driven by differences in local quota allocation practices, sales crediting practices and rep deployment. The worldwide sales leader ought to examine and discuss these results with their geo leads and ensure the company follows consistent practices for quota allocation.

By Tenure. Another important data cut is by tenure. More tenured reps often have a better chance of exceeding quota. This shouldn't be the case. While new hires have understandable ramp-up times, fully onboarded new hires should have similar quota distributions as tenured hires. However, they often don't. Managers tend to allocate less than they should to tenured, strong performers, and more than they should to new hires. The sales leader must watch for and mitigate this practice. Good data sheds light on the situation and drives the right conversation.

By Job Role. Hunter, farmer, account manager, overlay, first-line manager. Should different job roles have the same quota distributions? Maybe not, but all of these job role distributions should be balanced and centered around the 100% attainment mark. The standard deviations may be different. For example, account manager (i.e., "farmer") roles in mature, well-established markets (e.g., office products) will have much smaller standard deviations (customers can only buy so many more paper clips). Meanwhile, account executives (i.e., "hunters") in fast-growing new markets (e.g., cloud computing) will have much larger standard deviations. Don't try to manage the standard deviations–doing so will lead to artificially manipulating pay. Instead, test and manage for displaced, multimodal and overall skewed results.

Get Started! When it comes to quotas, there's a lot at stake. Analysis of quota performance distributions yields a wide range of insights to improve the quality of your quota program and thus the performance and health of the sales force and the ROI on your sales investment. Determine which sub-groups to review based on the structure of your organization and your sense for specific problem and opportunity areas. From there, you can formulate hypotheses about root causes, dig deeper where needed, and more importantly, change how you set goals next year.

Get Confident About Setting New Product Quotas: 5 Things to Consider

Setting accurate quotas is tough. It tops the list of challenges for most sales leaders. However, what's even more challenging than setting accurate quotas? Assigning quotas for a new product. With new products, you have even less to work with–no historical sales data or performance data. How do companies do this, and do it well?

Unfortunately, there is no simple formula. However, here are five fundamental factors you should consider each time you launch a new product and want to assign responsibility to the sales force to go out and sell it.

1. **Strategic Importance.** Is the new product "the big bet" for the organization? If the success of the organization depends on the new product's success, then you'll want to set aggressive goals, and be prepared to enable the sales force to succeed. Your primary sellers should have a "carve out" from their target incentive (TI) based roughly on how much time and attention you want them to give the new product. A carve out of 15% to 20% is a start.

Predictably, allocating 40% or greater of the target incentive will garner serious seller attention.

Characteristics	FIVE FACTORS	Characteristics
LOW • Modest quota increase	**STRATEGIC IMPORTANCE**	**HIGH** • Aggressive quota increase • >40% TI carve-out • Sales force enablement
Similar, adjacent or line extension • Modest quota increase	**PRODUCT SIMILARITY**	**New, different** • Aggressive quota increase • >20% TI carve-out • Product specialists
Same • Modest quota increase	**TARGET BUYER**	**Different** • Aggressive quota increase • >20% TI carve-out • Updated sales process • New selling skills
Similar • Modest quota increase	**BUYING PROCESS**	**Different** • Modest quota increase • Product specialists • Overlay
Few • Modest quota increase	**SALES BAG CAPACITY**	**Many** • Aggressive quota increase • >20% TI carve-out

2. **Product Similarity.** What is the nature of the new product? Is it a line extension, an adjacent or complementary offering? If it's similar, and the seller can easily understand it and sell it along with existing products, then a modest increase in quotas to reflect the new product potential is likely enough. If the product is significantly different, particularly if it's more complex, simply raising quotas may not work. Reps may need additional training and enablement, including deploying overlay product specialists who are tied 100% to the new product. To drive core rep focus, carve out TI and assign a portion of it to the new product quota.

3. **Target Buyer.** Is the new product something you see your reps selling to their existing buyers? Or, is it intended for a different target buyer? If the new product is a complement to the current suite of products, then adoption is often smoother. Modest increases in quotas for your core reps may do the trick to capture the added opportunity in each sales rep's bag. However, if the new product is for a new buyer, get ready for resistance. Your top sellers will

typically "get it," particularly if the average sales price for the new product is significantly higher than their current go-to. However, your core sellers will likely remain entrenched and will resort to comfort-zone selling. Selling this new product requires bigger behavioral change. This may entail support and enablement in the form of updating the sales process, selling skills and overlay resources like product specialists. And, the new product quotas may need to be "carved out" of TI (20% or more) to garner enough attention.

4. **Buying Process.** What is the process for selling the new product? Is it similar to existing products? Do you believe it will have a similar sales cycle? If the process is similar to your existing products, it should be easier to integrate and therefore easier for your reps to sell. Modest quota adjustments should be sufficient. However, if the buying process is quite different–particularly if it's longer and more complex—just adding quota will likely not work. The company may need to focus new product quota on overlay roles like new product specialists, and introduce it gradually in to core rep quotas. Depending on the importance of the new product, you may consider offering a multiplier on new product sales or a higher acceleration rate beyond quota once the seller achieves the new product target.

5. **Sales Bag Capacity.** How full is your sales rep's sales bag? The number of products in the sales rep's bag can have an impact on how much focus the new product gets. If a sales rep already has a large suite of products, the new addition may get lost in the shuffle. To drive focus, it's common to set aggressive goals and get the rep's attention. Conversely, if the new product is only a second or third offering you're adding to the rep's bag, the focus is almost unavoidable. In this scenario, the new product quota will likely be a significant portion of a rep's overall quota.

If setting quotas is tough, then setting new product quotas can be downright scary. However, careful consideration of several key factors should help you make sound decisions. As we've shown, it's not always the best strategy to press ahead aggressively or to timidly approach quota allocation year over year. Every sales organization struggles with quota setting. It will always be part art/part science. Consider these five factors when setting new product quotas and feel confident you've nailed the science part.

Industry Perspectives

Articles in Section

❖

5 Key Technology and XaaS Sales Compensation Challenges

How Are You Measuring Your Cloud Sales Representatives?

Media Sales: Sales Compensation for Covert Versus
Overt Account Managers

Setting Target Total Compensation Levels:
A Digital Media/SaaS Company Story

Sales Compensation Issues and Solutions for Media Ad Sales

Link or Sink: Sales Comp Strategy for Print Media Companies

Today's Manufacturing Sales Teams: How to 'Lean' the Sales
Compensation Program

Sales Compensation Considerations for Key Manufacturing Roles

Health Insurance: Sales Compensation Issues and Solutions

Medical Device: Sales Compensation Issues and Solutions

Distribution: Sales Compensation Issues and Solutions

5 Key Technology and XaaS Sales Compensation Challenges

Sales leaders responsible for go-to-customer strategy within the technology industry have much to contend with today. Market and product portfolio changes are happening a mile a minute. Buyers are changing, companies are merging/splitting, product roadmaps are evolving and customers are leveraging the information age to become more knowledgeable about their needs and vendor solutions.

Sales compensation is a key lever in driving performance within this rapidly changing environment. However, designing the right sales compensation plans in this complex tech world is full of challenges. This article identifies five key go-to-customer challenges:

1. Aligning pay for land, adopt, renew and expand sales motions

2. Hybrids: migrating towards XaaS from perpetual license/hardware

3. Compensating for enabling services (implementation, data migration, consulting and training)

4. Ensuring multiyear payouts align to strategy and financial goals

5. Sales compensation strategy in a consumption pricing model

1. Aligning pay for land, adopt, renew and expand sales motions. XaaS companies are responsible for four key sales motions–landing new customers, ensuring the customers adopt the solution and recognize value immediately, renewing the customer's business through a renewal contract or ongoing payment, and expanding their opportunity via upsell and cross-sell opportunities. These sales motions are four different measures, each with its own level of strategic focus and effort. Even if different roles own different sales motions, leaders must make critical decisions on how best to drive focus while keeping the plan simple.

2. Hybrids: migrating towards XaaS from perpetual license/hardware. Most traditional perpetual license and hardware companies are migrating towards XaaS solutions. XaaS solutions typically provide less quota credit than the traditional solution, causing misaligned seller focus. Typical solution options include measures, crediting rules, value adjustments and hurdles. However, leaders can get stuck with no clear migration strategy, varied migration strategies by product and keeping the plan simple.

3. Compensating for enabling services (implementation, data migration, consulting and training). Most companies are in the business of selling a solution. To ensure the solution is deployed and used correctly, companies offer implementation services, data migration, professional consulting contracts and training. Most organizations realize lower margins for these solutions and leverage partners to provide them. Leaders must determine how much sales compensation emphasis to put on these services for each sales role.

4. Ensuring multiyear payouts align to strategy and financial goals. Any ongoing service, such as maintenance contracts for perpetual licenses, break and fix service contracts, or XaaS solutions, typically include a term length. Here's the conundrum: Is a three-year $100k deal worth the same as three separate $100k deals, each with its own lifetime value? Typically, no. It is difficult to accurately set total contract value quotas when term lengths vary. Leaders must select the right measure(s), crediting rule(s) and mechanic(s) to align payouts with their multiyear strategy in a cost-efficient manner.

5. Sales compensation strategy in a consumption pricing model. Best-in-class sales compensation plans follow the "pay for persuasion" principle, where the plan pays for closing a contract via a bookings or billings event. Persuasion events vary in a consumption pay-as-you-go pricing model: first at the time of contract close, then as the customer uses/pays for the offering into the future. Leaders must figure out the right measure, crediting event and time duration.

These five key challenges will vary by company depending on their product portfolio, coverage model and job roles. Best-in-class companies assemble multifunctional design teams to tease out the applicable options and decide on the simplest plan that drives their strategy.

How Are You Measuring Your Cloud Sales Representatives?

Selecting the right measures is the most important decision when developing a sales compensation plan. The sales compensation plan performance measures and measure weights provide clear direction to the sales rep on what to focus on and how much time to focus on it. This is a particularly challenging objective for the incentive plan of cloud sales representatives.

DO YOU HAVE A CLEAR STRATEGY AND ROLES?

Before selecting measures, confirm the company strategy and desired sales behaviors for each selling role. If the strategy is ill-defined and/or the job role is unclear, corrupted or unfocused, then two problems can occur. First, the sales comp plan can drive the wrong behavior. For example, one cloud company decided to remove renewals from its account executive (AE) plans since a separate role was going to focus on renewal sales. However, two years into this approach, the renewal rate had dropped by 10%. Removing the AE's focus on renewals had a direct impact on renewal rates. The second problem, which often occurs when the strategy or roles are ill-defined, is unnecessary long sales compensation plan design cycles. In one case, a hybrid on-premise/cloud software company spent four months going back and forth on measures and weights for its sales reps, who sold both on-premise and cloud solutions, because leadership could not decide what to prioritize.

WHAT MEASURE(S) TO USE?

There are many different cloud (or recurring revenue business model) measures that companies use. The following list provides a short list of these measures. The business type focus (new, renewal, total) depends on the role definition. How much time is the role hunting in the wild, hunting in the zoo or farming? The use of booking metrics (ACV, TCV, MRR), revenue metrics (TBR, Revenue) or number of deals depends on the company's business model and contract commitment level. The Alexander Group's Cloud Sales Index Study of 22 pure play cloud and hybrid companies indicates 100% of the companies use bookings, followed by revenue (41%), multiyear (35%) and net recurring revenue (29%). Other measures include number of new accounts, cash up-front and retention.

Cloud/Recurring Revenue Measure Types

Contract Value	Recurring Revenue	Billed Revenue	Existing Business/ Renewals	# of Deals
• Annual Contract Value (ACV) • Total Contract Value (TCV) • Net New Bookings (NNB)	• Annual Recurring Revenue (ARR) • Monthly Recurring Revenue (MRR) • Net Recurring Revenue (NRR)	• Total Billed Revenue (TBR) • Total Billings • Total Portfolio Net Revenue • Total Revenue • Net Revenue	• Renewals • Churn • Renewal Rate • Sales to Existing Customers	• New Logo • New Deal Bonus • Number of Logos • Contract Signing Bonus

In general, companies should measure and credit a sales rep as close as possible to the persuasion event, usually when the customer signs a contract. However, a few situations call for crediting the sales rep on downstream events like invoice, delivery, customer acceptance or cash collection. For technology and cloud companies, the measure selection and crediting decision depends on the company's business model and contract commitment level. The following framework outlines the crediting considerations for each business model and commitment level. For example, perpetual license sales with an absolute commitment are credited at the time of bookings or invoice (invoice is generally done at the time of bookings, so it is a proxy for bookings). Subscription models generally credit a committed value at time of bookings, and utility models generally pay on actual usage. Because the crediting event for utility models occurs after the bookings event (and in many cases, way after the bookings event), compensation plans for utility models often include some type of number of deals measure.

Just over half of the companies in our Cloud Sales Index Study credit at bookings (56%), followed by invoice (24%), deployment (8%), delivery/usage (4%), various stages (4%) and other (4%). For contracts with varying term lengths, annual contract value (ACV) is the most predominant practice (54%), followed by total contract value (TCV) (38%), net present value (NPV) (4%) and decelerated value (4%). Other practices we have seen include total value staggered and first-year value only. The most common reason for using ACV over TCV is to accommodate unpredictable contract term lengths that cause quota-setting issues (i.e., when term lengths vary, ACV makes it easier to predict performance expectations and set quotas). For plans based on ACV, it's not uncommon to also have a measure to recognize and reward for multiyear deals. This could come in the form of a credit uplift, an add-on incentive or a separate multiyear measure.

Technology Sales Crediting Framework

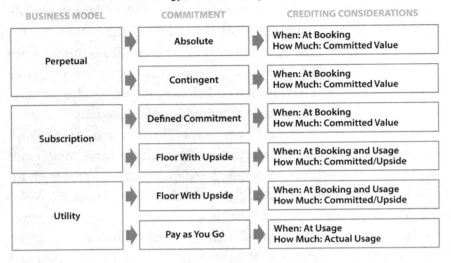

BUSINESS MODEL	COMMITMENT	CREDITING CONSIDERATIONS
Perpetual	Absolute	When: At Booking / How Much: Committed Value
Perpetual	Contingent	When: At Booking / How Much: Committed Value
Subscription	Defined Commitment	When: At Booking / How Much: Committed Value
Subscription	Floor With Upside	When: At Booking and Usage / How Much: Committed/Upside
Utility	Floor With Upside	When: At Booking and Usage / How Much: Committed/Upside
Utility	Pay as You Go	When: At Usage / How Much: Actual Usage

HOW MANY MEASURES?

Best practice is to keep the plan simple with three or fewer measures. Too many measures dilute sales representative focus and complicate incentive calculations. With more than three measures, representatives tend to "fog out" and just do what seems best rather than pay attention to the sales compensation plan. In our recent study, 95% of participants use three or fewer measures, with 82% using only one or two measures.

WHAT PERFORMANCE MEASURE WEIGHTS TO USE?

When leadership wants to drive multiple strategic objectives and, in particular, when specific roles have multiple goals, it becomes necessary to have two or three measures in the compensation plan. The next key decision is how to break down a sales rep's target incentive across those measures in the form of a measure weight (e.g., 70% new business and 30% renewal business). Best practice is to think of how much time you want your sales rep spending on each measure and the strategic importance of each measure. Quota size should not drive this decision. For example, a hybrid software/cloud company wanted to place more emphasis on new business over existing business. When they looked at the quota sizes, each rep's book of business varied dramatically between high new (80% new) to mixed bag (50% new and 50% renewal) to high renewal (70%-plus renewal). They created three plan designs to accommodate three books of business profiles. However, when they surveyed the sales force regarding their time allocation, 80% of their time was focused on new business regardless of how much renewal business they had, mainly due to the use of renewal reps to help focus on the renewal business. Thus, the company changed to one plan with 80% weighting on new and 20% on renewal, which simplified the plan design and aligned to the job's desired behaviors.

CLOSING

How are you measuring your cloud sales force? Is it driving the right behaviors? Are you achieving your strategic goals?

Media Sales:
Sales Compensation for Covert
Versus Overt Account Managers

Media advertising leaders need to define clearly their account manager sales roles. Specifically, are the account managers covert or overt sellers? What does this distinction mean? How does it affect the account manager's sales compensation plan design? Leaders who clearly articulate the role's involvement throughout the customer engagement process will improve job focus and can better align their sales compensation plans.

ACCOUNT MANAGER ROLE

Media leaders often pair account managers (AM), who are typically hybrid sales and service roles, with account executives (AE), who are the primary sellers and quota owners. AM roles are typically responsible for working with advertising operations to oversee media campaign setup and execution, optimizing media advertising spend, identifying upsell and cross-sell opportunities, and/or working with the AE to develop new customer pitches.

In media ad sales, there are four key sales motions: land new customers, expand business with current customers, renew current deals with current customers, and optimize current media ad spend/campaigns. The following chart includes four key sales motions and a visual representation of the AE and AM time across these motions. Although both roles play a part across all sales motions, the AE spends more time on land and expand, and the AM spends more time on renew and optimize. Leaders ultimately want the AM to focus on managing the daily RFP responses/media optimization so that the AE has time to focus on chief marketing officer/budget-maker activities.

Land	Expand	Renew	Optimize
Account Executive			
			Account Manager

COVERT VERSUS OVERT SELLING RESPONSIBILITY

When it comes to sales execution, leaders can design either covert or overt AMs.

Covert AMs are responsible for identifying sales opportunities and creating a solution, which they pass off to an AE to close the deal. Companies use covert AMs when they need the AM to be a trusted service delivery resource. However, in this model, the AE must spend significant time supporting all sales opportunities, including smaller/incremental deals as opposed to focusing the majority of time working with the chief marketing officer on major budget spending.

Meanwhile, overt AMs are responsible for closing smaller upsell/cross-sell deals and/or driving incremental spend. Companies use overt AMs when they want their AEs to focus on more CMO/budget-setting activities and when the AMs have true sales capabilities (career path to an AE role). However, overt AMs are more expensive and can increase the COS if they do not drive incremental revenue.

SALES COMPENSATION PLAN IMPACT

There are four primary sales compensation components to consider when designing AM sales compensation plans.

1. **Pay Levels.** Companies set pay levels using market labor pay data aligned to their pay philosophy and target market. Covert AMs are less expensive than overt AMs. Companies must ensure that they are mapping to the right market benchmark job when pricing these jobs.

2. **Pay Mix.** Pay mix is a ratio of base salary versus target incentive (TI) as a percent of target total compensation (TTC). The role's degree of sales persuasion/influence determines the amount of pay at risk. As the role's level of persuasion/influence over a sale increases, so should the percent of TTC coming from the TI. As shown in the following chart, overt AMs tend to have a more

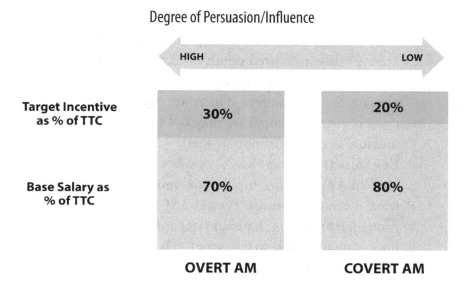

aggressive 70/30 pay mix, whereas covert AMs have less aggressive 80/20 pay mixes.

3. **Leverage.** Leverage is the amount of variable pay awarded to the top 90th percentile performer expressed as a ratio of target incentive (e.g., 2x). Most sales roles have a 3x leverage. Therefore, the more selling time (versus non-selling time like servicing or marketing), the higher leverage a role has. As shown in the following chart, overt AMs have more sales time and therefore are eligible for a higher leverage (2x) than covert AMs (1.5x).

Selling Time Versus Non-Selling Time

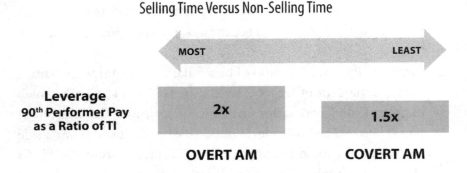

4. **Measures.** Companies typically use two types of measures to reward AM performance within a sales compensation plan.
   - **Total Revenue (Overlay Metric).** Both overt and covert AMs are typically measured on an overlay revenue metric. The AM's revenue metric is usually based on the AEs whom they are assigned to. However, if there are significant AM and AE reassignments, companies may opt to use a team revenue measure (e.g., district or manager).
   - **Key Sales Objectives (KSOs).** KSOs are effective to measure how an AM executes his/her job and/or when they deploy team revenue measures. Typical AM KSOs include on-time campaign execution, renewal rates and account growth. It is important to be able to measure KSOs in order to implement them effectively.

Successful media advertising companies leverage AM roles to drive revenue growth. First, they need to effectively design the role and then develop the appropriate sales compensation plan. If an AM role evolves from covert selling to overt selling, sales leadership should review the sales compensation plan and update accordingly.

Setting Target Total Compensation Levels: A Digital Media/ SaaS Company Story

The art of pricing sales jobs begins with benchmarking target total compensation to market data. Companies should follow a best-in-class process to set and manage their pay structures.

Setting new sales job pay structures can take one to two months depending on the number of jobs and incumbents. For many companies, following a typical best practices process may suffice (see Figure 1).

What if a company faces more challenging data situations? An Alexander Group (AGI) engagement with a digital media ad sales and SaaS client offers clues for managing complex pay structures.

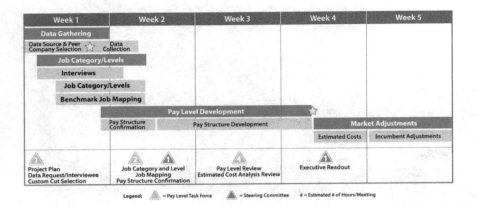

FIGURE 1: Pay Level Setting Timeline

DATA GATHERING

First, gather all current data and job information. Research available survey sources and select the most appropriate sources. Select a custom cut of data.

Client Issue: A digital ad sales company just launched a SaaS solution. What data set should it use?

Client Solution: AGI selected two separate custom data cuts to understand how each market pays: one set of digital media ad sales companies, and one set of SaaS companies that sell to sales and marketing organizations.

Client Issue: Limited data in some countries.

Client Solution: Compared market variance between custom cut data with general software industry cut in countries with high n-counts. Next, applied the variance to the general software cut in countries with low n-counts.

Interview sales leaders to clarify job content for more accurate job mapping. Make sure to ask questions around internal job equity when accurate job matches are not available. Articulate job levels by job family and map to survey levels (see Figure 2). This structure provides the basis for creating the new pay levels.

Client Issue: Inadequate job matches for many jobs. For example, the survey source had a sales representative job, but the client had separate hunters and farmers. In addition, the survey source did not have a good digital media account manager role.

Client Solution: Compared market variance between hunters and farmers in the general software cut, then applied the variance to the digital media roles. Leveraged a similar role used in the software industry and applied it to digital media.

#	Company Job Families and Levels				Survey Levels	
	Account Executive	Sales Management	Account Manager	AM Management	Survey IC Levels	Survey Mgmt Levels
12	SVP Advertising Solutions					SVP
11	Sales VP					VP
10		Sr. Dir, Sales Management		Sr. Dir, Account Management		6
9		Dir, Sales Management		Dir, Account Management	N/A	5
8	Account Executive Expert	Sr. Mgr, Sales Management		Sr. Mgr, Account Management	5	4
7	Account Executive Advanced	Mgr, Sales Management	Account Manager Advanced	Mgr, Account Management	4	3
6	Account Executive Senior		Sales Marketing Manager Senior		3	
5	Account Executive Staff		Sales Marketing Manager Staff		2	
4			Sales Marketing Manager Associate		1	

Source: Anonymized AGI Client

FIGURE 2: Job Families and Levels

PAY LEVEL DEVELOPMENT

Clarify pay philosophy and pay structure practices. Next, create an Excel workbook and gather all the market data to set a pay structure for each job/level for each country.

Client Issue: Must review multiple data sources and jobs to set structure for each job. In addition, needed to apply variance ratios to many jobs. Lastly, some market data was suspect (e.g., higher job levels paid lower and big pay jumps between levels).

Client Solution: Create a robust Excel workbook. Create a tab for each job family and pull in all data sources (industry cut, jobs and levels). This meant pulling 20-plus rows of data. Although company mapped to 50th percentile, pull in multiple percentiles (e.g., 25th, 50th and 75th). Calculate ratios to the side. Graphically display all data in a stock chart to visualize and synthesize the full view. Leverage all data inputs to set new pay structures within each job family tab.

MARKET ADJUSTMENTS

Once complete, analyze compa-ratios for each incumbent. If there is a need to make market adjustments, set a market adjustment budget for each leader to use to make adjustments. Set market adjustment budgets by analyzing two scenarios: 1) Move all incumbents, who are below the minimum of the range, to the minimum point of the new structure. 2) Move all incumbents, who are below the minimum of the range, to the mid-point of the new structure. Next, set a budget between those two points. HR/comp should work closely with sales leaders and the HR business partners to review each individual's situation and make market adjustments based on employee performance and value to the firm.

Client Problem: Market corrections were expensive. Must obtain executive buy-off on the budget impact.

Client Solution: AGI leveraged its COS benchmark database and turnover/ramping employee costs to justify the market adjustment costs.

CONCLUSION

Analyzing market data to develop pay structures is not always a straightforward exercise. Sophisticated sales compensation professionals should be able to triangulate across multiple data elements to drive sound pay level decisions to attract and retain the right talent for their company.

Sales Compensation Issues and Solutions for Media Ad Sales

The changing media landscape will require major selling changes. Ad customers are demanding measurable ROI offerings across multiple products and devices. The proliferation of programmatic ad buying, multiplatform solutions and all-things mobile is causing disruption in the online marketplace. Sales leaders are making tough go-to-customer selling decisions, constantly placing bets on how to sell the diversity of ad products to different customer segments. A transformative approach to solution selling offers media organizations a better opportunity to thrive in this changing landscape.

Changing sales modes requires frequent updates to sales compensation plans to ensure alignment between sales efforts and selling strategies.

Through our benchmark research, observations from our Media Advisory Council and active engagement with clients, the Alexander

Group (AGI) has identified two prominent sales compensation challenges:

1. Paying for solution selling

2. Rewarding pre- and post-sales support roles

PAYING FOR SOLUTION SELLING

Advertisers today demand that publishers provide a diverse product portfolio and the ability to measure return on investment (ROI). Publishers have responded by increasing the size of their product portfolios. This additional investment in new products enables ad sales organizations to achieve their clients' goals.

The investment and introduction of multiple products will continue. However, 88% of participants in the AGI Media Study noted they were struggling to configure sales compensation plans to drive solution selling. Most sales leaders are stymied by challenges related to goal setting, differentiating between high and low performers and fostering team collaboration.

However, many media companies are making a variety of sales compensation adjustments to pay for solution selling:

- Less aggressive pay mix for account executives as they focus on long-term, more strategic solution selling

- Increased use of focused product measures and mechanics (e.g., value adjustments and hurdles)

- Plan alignment with new roles (e.g., global, agency holding company, MM inside, programmatic)

- Increased use of varied accelerator rates based on quota bands to equalize upside opportunity

As the solution portfolio grows supporting advertiser expectations, the account executive role requires more pre- and post- sales support. These resources enable account executives (AE) to expand their sales capacity and focus across the portfolio. Pre-sales and marketing roles such as insights/research and customer solutions inform top of the funnel sales activities. On the post-sales side, ad ops and campaign measurement roles relieve the AE from fulfillment activities and provide buyer support campaign delivery (see the following figure).

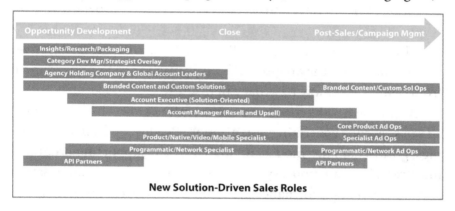

New Solution-Driven Sales Roles

Revenue leaders want all parties aligned to deliver the best possible solution for the client. Enablement Performance Plans provide incentive rewards for these non-sales roles (see the following figure).

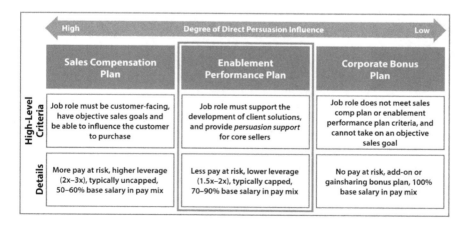

The enablement performance plan measures reflect the following job responsibilities.

Total Revenue Overlay Measure. When companies directly assign roles to an AE, the role is typically measured on the revenue they support. However, if there are significant AE reassignments, companies may opt to use a level-up team revenue measure (e.g., district or manager).

Key Sales Objectives (KSOs). KSOs are effective to measure non-revenue job responsibilities. Typical KSOs include on-time campaign execution, renewal rates and account growth. KSOs provide a flexible solution that allows leaders to tailor sales goals/initiatives by role or even by individual. Although sellers must focus on these objectives to earn incentive, they require effective governance to prevent them from being a giveaway or "salary in disguise."

As the media advertising industry continues to evolve, so must the ad sales revenue generating organization. Product and solution offerings, go-to-customer model and management supporting programs must remain contemporary to remain relevant. Sales compensation and enablement performance plans are critical levers for driving the right behaviors to not only survive, but thrive in today's environment.

Link or Sink: Sales Comp Strategy for Print Media Companies

Media advertising sales compensation programs can be the difference between winning or losing in the digital age.

Today's dynamic media landscape requires integrated print companies to continually question and reinvent their go-to-customer models. These companies generate revenue from both print as well as digital advertising and other visibility offerings. Media companies must leverage every sales management tool available to remain competitive, including the sales compensation program.

Using a "linked" sales compensation formula design is one approach to ensure integrated, balanced selling of all service offerings. Digital solutions selling is generally far more complex than traditional print solutions. As such, they are outside the comfort zone of many incumbent sales representatives. Digital solutions often require a smaller monetary investment than traditional print offerings on a spend-per-campaign basis. This dynamic causes friction between total revenue (i.e., "what keeps the lights on") and digital revenue (i.e., "the future of the business"). Digital is the undeniable future of media advertising; sales compensation is a mechanism for balancing priorities.

In the following illustrative example, ABC Media has created a sales compensation program for its core sales representatives, which includes two measures: one for total revenue weighted at 70% and one for digital revenue weighted at 30%. The measure weightings reflect the balance placed on total revenue versus digital to sustain a profitable business while keeping an eye on the future. Revenue leadership sets independent goals for each measure. Every dollar of digital revenue attainment also counts toward the total revenue measure. In order for sellers to maximize their above-goal earnings on total revenue, they must achieve their digital sales results. In this case, the incentive link threshold is set at 100% of the digital revenue performance goal.

ABC Media Company Core Sales Representative Compensation Plan Measure & Link Illustration

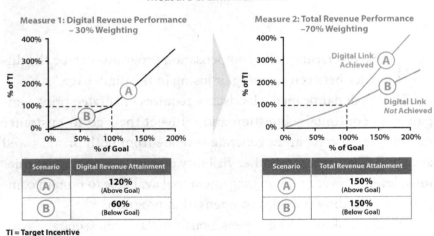

TI = Target Incentive

The digital link communicates to the sales force that while total revenue is important and highly weighted, achieving the digital performance threshold is necessary in order to maximize total incentive earnings. The link can also work inversely if the sales compensation program design more heavily weights digital versus total revenue. Of course, sound strategy and sales compensation design alone are not sufficient for successful change adoption. Therefore, there are a few "musts" to ensure the success of a linked sales compensation program. Organizations:

- Must obtain buy-in from sales management, particularly the first-line sales leaders, in advance of rolling out the new program.

- Must provide tools (e.g., Excel-based calculators) to illustrate how the linked design works and how to win with the new program.

- Must keep in mind that sales compensation is only one element of effective sales management. It will not solve for all challenges.

- Must clearly communicate to the sales force what has changed and why, as well as answer the question, "What's in it for me?"

Today's Manufacturing Sales Teams: How to 'Lean' the Sales Compensation Program

Traditional manufacturing sales teams drove sales success with relationship development and feature-benefit product knowledge. Today, most sales teams are rapidly advancing toward more consultative, collaborative selling models. As with any change in the sales model, the sales compensation plan faces an inevitable shock. The old incentive plan no longer supports the new selling approach. Sales leaders can use lean management concepts to better align the pay program to the emerging sales models.

SALES TEAMS OF THE FUTURE

Manufacturers are facing decreased competitive product cycle times erasing first mover or technical competitive advantage. Sales functions need to develop global processes, increased scale and multiproduct coordination. Successful sales teams are now embracing their customers' non-linear buying journey. New customer access methods such as digital engagement allow sellers and marketing teams to meet influencers and buyers on their terms. New sales models feature fewer, deeper, more intelligent relationships with their channel partners.

The good news is you can realign your sales pay program using the lean management discipline, including embracing seller focus changes, reducing distractions and a willingness to adjust to changing business circumstances and marketplace challenges.

LEAN SOLUTIONS

A lean sales compensation program clears the clutter of poorly designed, misaligned and obsolete incentive plans. By drawing on existing improvement concepts found in manufacturing entities, you can create a lasting program that delivers ROI through a disciplined approach.

The "leaning" of sales compensation can borrow traditional lean constructs. By embracing a continuous improvement process, astute sales executives can develop compensation models that best serve their organization's current sales objectives. The key here is to take a consistent, long-term approach to sales compensation alignment, rather than a one-off quick fix.

WHY PEOPLE MATTER

Ultimately, changes to the sales compensation plan affect employees, your sellers. Engage the right team. Seek field contributions. Sales leaders need to solicit insight from field sales managers. Listen to sellers' opinions. (However, be careful . . . every seller thinks he or she is underpaid). Use a multifaceted design team, including HR, sales operations, finance and IT.

Provide assurance to your sellers that you are not reducing the overall sales compensation budget, but making changes to bring alignment to seller efforts and current sales objectives. Sure, the sales compensation plans might change how sellers are paid, but confirm that individuals can earn equal or greater levels of pay with the new plans. It is a formula for a winning outcome for both the sales culture and sales results.

Remember the No. 1 cause for sales compensation plan failure is loss of hope. Ensure every seller has the chance and opportunity to earn his/her target compensation and more.

SUCCESSFUL PROGRAM ADOPTION

Your implementation team should be immersed in the sales world. Seek out conditions that will both aid and hurt implementation of the new pay plan. Sales leadership must prepare their sales team for the impending change, putting a spotlight on potential rewards and opportunities.

Use multiple communication techniques, including leadership speeches, webinars, one-on-one personalized discussions and breaking news stories, to share the excitement of the new compensation program, as well as how sellers and the company will benefit.

NAVIGATING YOUR NEW SALES COMPENSATION FUTURE

When you are ready to "lean" your sales compensation program, it's important to commit to a process and build the muscle memory you'll need to communicate and educate your teams. You will want to conduct an in-depth review of your sales compensation plans annually. Challenges and opportunities will continue. The realignment of sales compensation should keep pace with the evolving assigned strategy of the sales function.

Sales Compensation Considerations for Key Manufacturing Roles

Sales compensation in the manufacturing sector has unique characteristics due to multiple routes by which companies deliver products to market through both direct and indirect channels (distributors). Although manufacturers are aware of what their direct channel accounts are selling, they have limited insight into end-user data when a distributor makes the sale. In an environment where obtaining true end-user customer data is a common challenge, sales leadership should pay particular attention to two core plan components to ensure that the sales compensation plan still pays for sales performance: pay mix and plan measures. To demonstrate the impact of data limitations on these plan components, we will use two core sales roles in the manufacturing industry as examples, territory sellers and corporate account managers.

PAY MIX

Companies define pay mix as the percentage of target total compensation expressed in the form of base pay/incentive pay, e.g., $60K base with a $40K target incentive results in a 60/40 pay mix. Pay mix reflects the job's degree of individual customer or business partner persuasion. New factors that influence pay mix are a role's level of revenue influence and the job role's strategic focus.

Both territory sellers and corporate account managers tend to have a more conservative pay mix due to the nature of the job roles and limitations of data. Territory sellers have a less aggressive pay mix when aligned to an indirect channel as a result of limitations in obtaining actual point-of-sale data. Since corporate account managers typically work on accounts/opportunities with longer sales cycles, they also tend to have a conservative pay mix. Typically, pay mix for these roles falls between 70/30 and 85/15. A pay mix in this range allows the sellers to have some portion of their pay at risk; however, it does account for the fact that actual end-user sales data is limited.

PLAN MEASURES

The next challenge when designing plans where point-of-sale data is lacking is deciding on what measure to use in the plan. With the inclusion of a distributor, receiving end-user customer data is challenging, which impacts how to "measure" sellers. Typically, measures for these roles fall into two categories: sales measures and management by objectives (MBOs). MBOs drive business outcomes, but companies are unable to track them without sales-related data.

Territory sellers are removed from the end-user, so it is difficult to tie sales efforts to results. A common option for compensating this type of sales role is to tie incentive solely to sales growth in the territory rather than trying to gather end-user account level sales data. While point-of-sale data would provide insight to the end-user, sales within the territory can serve as a proxy. This plan measure rewards sellers by aligning their efforts with the distributors to generate sales with end-users.

Sales management can also elect to include an MBO in a territory seller's compensation plan as a secondary measure. This provides another avenue for sales leadership to put focus on areas that are unrelated to sales results. MBOs drive business outcomes that cannot be tracked with revenue.

For the corporate account manager roles, plan metrics can vary depending on the ability to get accurate point-of-sale data from the corporate account. If manufacturers can obtain sales data on corporate accounts, they can elect to compensate sellers on this number. At times, even though corporate accounts buy through an indirect channel, a manufacturer can get more granular data due to the corporate relationship. This gives sellers direct line-of-sight to the performance measure on which companies compensate them. There is a direct correlation between sales results and incentive compensation earned.

Similar to the territory seller role, corporate account manager plans can include MBOs. The MBOs can provide sales incentive for items, such as sales process milestones, which are critical steps in a long sales process. However, using a plan based solely on MBOs does not align with the concept of tying sales results to incentive payments. Ideally, a revenue-/sales-based measure should be the primary measure in a corporate account manager plan.

Regardless of which channels a manufacturer uses, understanding the limitations of data is critical in designing the right sales compensation plan. Sales data might not be readily available, but sellers will still need to have some metric for measurement for sales incentive compensation. Therefore, the absence of end-user point-of-sales data does not mean manufacturers cannot create an effective and motivating sales compensation plan.

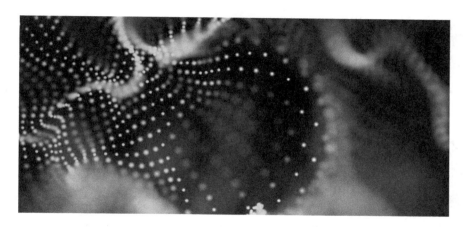

Sales Compensation Issues
and Solutions

The health insurance industry is experiencing uncertain times: changing competitor participants, regulatory/government turmoil, changes in healthcare products and evolving buyer expectations.

These factors place increased pressure on health insurance carriers to think carefully about future strategies for attracting, retaining and motivating the sales force. The sales compensation plan is a critical tool for translating strategy into sales behaviors and outcomes.

Let's examine three key contemporary issues and potential solutions for health insurance sales compensation:

No. 1: Insufficient focus on non-medical offerings (e.g., specialty/ancillaries, wellness)

No. 2: Legacy flat commission rate structures that limit the company's ability to drive growth

No. 3: Limited or no emphasis on profitability in sales compensation plans

No. 1: Insufficient focus on non-medical offerings (e.g., specialty/ancillaries, wellness).

Issue. As traditional products come under pressure from competition and self-funded programs, carriers need to embrace new products, including dental, vision, life insurance, wellness products and others. These products drive higher customer retention and profitability. However, many industry players have been slow to upgrade and offer these specialty products for cross-selling opportunities. Compounding this problem, many carriers place a minor focus on these offerings in the sales compensation plan. This results in representatives ignoring them and still earning incentives.

Solution. Determine the right blend of "carrot and stick." Carve out a separate performance measure for specialty products, introduce quota credit or payout rate multipliers, or provide add-on bonuses. These options provide different carrot versus stick implications. Also, consider your ability to set goals for these non-medical products. Some options require more accurate goal setting, while others do not require any goals. Due to the smaller volumes associated with non-medical products, companies provide greater emphasis in the sales compensation plan by using a specific mechanism to motivate representatives.

No. 2: Legacy flat commission rate structures that limit the company's ability to drive growth.

Issue. In the past, health insurance sales compensation plans mostly featured flat commission rates (traditional "rate card" plans). Today, companies use a mix of flat commission rates and goal-based bonus plans as they embrace a higher level of pay-for-performance and pay-for-growth philosophies. Flat commission rates severely limit the company's ability to drive year-over-year growth results. Representatives simply determine a desired target income that has minimal linkage to supporting company growth objectives. By migrating to more goal-oriented or goal-based plan structures, carriers take the reins on growth and direct representatives to ensure payouts align with growth objectives.

Solutions.

1. Introduce a goal achievement bonus alongside a straight commission-based plan. Companies can easily add this to a commission-based plan and inject a growth requirement to help align representative behavior with company growth goals.

2. Migrate to a fully goal-based compensation plan that directly links incentive pay to goal achievement. This solution pays a percentage of a job's targeted variable incentive amount for each increment of goal achievement, instead of a commission rate per contract or member. While this can be a big transition for companies with traditional commission structures, the payoff over time enables much stronger management of pay for performance.

3. Ensure goals reflect opportunity. Many companies set goals for representatives based on historical performance and assign a universal flat growth amount for the coming year. However, ignoring market opportunities in a territory can greatly underestimate or overestimate the goal for a particular representative. While determining sales potential, using opportunity data helps inform proper goal setting at the representative level. Carrier competitive intensity, rate plan strength/weakness in a market, provider access and network, and other factors are inputs to defining opportunity and improving representative goal setting.

No. 3: Limited or no emphasis on profitability in sales compensation plans.

Issue. A recent Alexander Group health insurance industry study revealed that 40% of surveyed companies (out of 30 study participants) have instituted some form of profitability into the sales compensation program for one or more roles. This represents a significant increase over previous years when profitability was very uncommon in sales compensation plans. Given current industry dynamics, carriers are facing more pressure to drive profitable sales while achieving growth objectives.

Solutions. There are three approaches to measuring profitability in a sales compensation plan: price realization/discount control, product emphasis and a margin metric. These mechanisms are on the rise as carriers take greater control of managing profit through the sales force.

1. **Price Realization/Discount Control.** A compensation measure to evaluate how close a deal comes to hitting the "target price" or "target discount" level. Some companies also choose to manage price/discounting through manager "concession pools." This allows sales managers to decide how to spend a bucket of dollars to strategically discount where needed and proactively manage profitability across customers.

2. **Product Emphasis.** Not all products are created equal. Providing additional quota credit or incentive pay for selling a more profitable product directly influences how representatives think about each opportunity. With the right plan design, this option drives significant profit increases through directed representative focus.

3. **Margin Metric.** The trickiest measure to get right is a margin metric because many elements are outside the control of the representative or manager. Carefully defining a margin metric to include only those elements influenced by the sales compensation plan

participant is important. Companies typically use this solution for sales management, where greater oversight and responsibility for margin components exists. Avoid the pitfall of including a company-level margin metric in representative or first-line management plans, because the line of sight is weak and incentive dollars go to waste.

Sales Compensation Issues and Solutions

Selling medical devices is undergoing a significant transformation. Traditionally, the seller's primary sales focus was selling to physicians. Sellers focused on driving physician preference for products. Sales representatives established tight-knit relationships with physicians. Medical device companies paid nicely for doctor determined purchases. The physician preference model treated sellers as income producers, who could take their physician relationships to a competitor. It was common for tenured sales representatives to earn greater than $400,000 to $500,000 from commission payouts.

The physician preference-selling model drove significant growth in the industry for many years, but two events significantly changed the medical device industry. First, the Great Recession (2007–2009) ushered in pricing pressures. Historically, 3% to 5% annual price increases were the norm, but for the first time hospitals not only rejected price increases, they mandated pricing concessions. Physician relationships could not ease hospitals' demands for lower prices.

Downward price pressures led to downward pressures on sales compensation. Up until this point, sales compensation programs largely featured very low base salaries with commission paid from dollar one-sales. Tenured sellers in large territories were the highest paid regardless of growth. Sales representatives essentially annuitized their physician relationships. The recession caused companies to rethink the pay-for-performance relationship and marked the end of dollar-one commission pay programs.

Second, the Affordable Care Act became law in 2009, which began an era focused on efficient care delivery and improved patient outcomes. The Affordable Care Act challenged the physician preference model. The hospital become the primary buyer, thus changing the go-to-customer model. This shift from physician-centric only selling to hospital and other stakeholder selling required a change in sales job design and, thus, the sales compensation program.

Medical device go-to-customer models have evolved from a single relationship-based physician focused model to a multifaceted buyer model. New models have to account for the needs of hospital systems, physicians, insurance companies and patients. To meet the needs of varied constituent buyer populations, new selling models employ a team-based approach. Today's customer-facing medical device sales organizations often include many of these roles:

- Key account managers: Communicate economic and clinical value to executives within large systems and major hospitals.

- Sales representatives: Maintain and expand relationships with physicians.

- Clinical specialists: Educate clinical stakeholders and cover surgical cases to improve product usage.

- Junior sales representatives: Provide superior service to high usage physicians; seller success leads to a full-fledged sales representative role.

- Managed care representatives: Ensures insurance reimbursement especially for procedures performed outside of the hospital.

- Field marketing: Develop customer-focused communication highlighting key value propositions.

The expansion in roles has put pressure on legacy compensation programs, and intensified the pressure on migrating from pay for volume to pay for performance. First step in the migration entails market-based pay levels. Team-based selling models require companies pay according to market values. In a market-based compensation model, sellers receive competitive compensation for achieving their quota. Today, medical device target pay ranges from approximately $120,000 annually to over $250,000 annually. Clinical complexity and intensity drive target pay levels. Generally, advanced cardiology and neurology products have the highest pay levels.

After establishing market pay levels, competitive pay mix (the ratio of base salary and target incentive as a percent of target total compensation) requires careful consideration. The medical device industry has evolved from almost no base salary to 50% base salary and 50% target incentive scheme. Additionally, base salaries are becoming a critical tactic in recruiting talent. The shift to greater base salaries accounts almost entirely the recent pay increases in the industry. Today's market for talent not only requires competitive total compensation, but also competitive base salaries.

Once sales management establishes competitive target compensation levels and pay mix ratios, a pay for performance compensation program needs to reward the "right" performance. For well-established products, the market has moved beyond volume-based only commission programs. The market now values growth and quota performance as the key determinant in incentive payouts for these products. For newer products, commission programs are still useful. However, commission programs are now used less. We recommend commission programs only where quotas are difficult to set. This situation typically arises for new or innovative products.

Based on Alexander Group industry studies, we expect sales compensation to continue to evolve across the industry. Continually evolving healthcare provider buying processes will exert pressure on both customer-facing jobs and sales compensation programs. In today's market, competitive pay that rewards for growth performance is the prevalent practice. The days of monetizing physician relationships are over. In today's world, sellers have to drive growth, and compensation programs are increasingly rewarding for sales growth.

Sales Compensation Issues
and Solutions

D istribution sales models continue to evolve at an accelerating
rate. Distribution sectors are increasingly consolidating as distributors acquire competitors to increase geographic reach, product breadth and strategic capabilities. Supplier strategies are shifting from broad and shallow to narrow and deep. Distributors need new jobs, new talent and new sales compensation plans.

Distribution leadership has several tools to drive sales force performance. One of the most powerful tools is the sales compensation program. Sales compensation models are changing in many ways: Sales quota methodologies are benefiting from newly available data sources, measures are becoming more tailored to specific growth strategies, and mechanics beyond commission plans are emerging. These changes allow sales leaders to be more prescriptive about sellers' efforts.

A good illustration of how these changes are affecting sales compensation is the shift of pay mix from high pay at-risk to more, lower pay-at risk.

BRIEF HISTORY OF PAY MIX IN DISTRIBUTION SALES MODELS

Pay mix expresses the ratio of base pay to variable pay at target performance. For example, if a seller's target total compensation (TTC) is $100,000 and the seller earns $60,000 in base and the remainder from variable pay, the seller has a 60/40 pay mix. In order to earn the $40,000 in variable, the seller must achieve 100% of the individual sales quota.

Traditional sales compensation plans for distributors use pay mixes that skew to more variable pay. 0/100 plans (zero base salary) existed, but pay plans more frequently featured pay mixes of 20/80 to 30/70 range. Management configured some of these pay plans with a recoverable draw instead of true base salaries. These plans offered unlimited upside to sellers, allowed organizations to minimize fixed compensation costs and attracted a self-focused seller. Low or no base plans worked well for organizations early in the growth cycle–white space was plentiful and sellers who sold as much as possible (regardless of customer type or product mix) were desirable and paid well for their efforts. The messaging to sellers on these types of plans was, "Hit your number, I don't care how you do it, and I'll pay you a fair rate on every dollar of gross profit." Sellers responded and created large books of business that produced consistent levels of spend year after year.

Eventually, sales strategies began to shift. Greater competition and margin pressures forced distributors to seek new pockets of growth. Shareholders and private equity firms handed down more aggressive growth targets. Product lines expanded and services (e.g., project management, inventory management, custom design) became increasingly important.

Sales leaders had a problem. The new strategies were not supported by legacy sales compensation plans. These plans with low base pay encourage sellers to act more like self-directed income producers than team member sales representatives.

Adjusting pay mix is a complex decision. Increasing the ratio of base pay to variable pay should allow more control over salespeople. Sellers should have to earn base pay by performing certain duties like any other salaried employee. Organizations could attract talent by offering better cash flow than traditional high-risk sales compensation plans. On the other hand, higher base salaries shift more budget into fixed costs. The associated reduction in variable pay at target (target incentive) worries sales leaders. They are concerned that plans with higher base pay, but reduced upside potential, will not attract the hunters who have traditionally been the top performers.

Before sales leaders go through with a change to pay mix, they must define how sellers earn base salary. Base salary is a useful tool to pay sellers for "table stakes" results that have been paid via commission in the past. These results include:

- Account and territory planning

- CRM data entry

- Pipeline reporting and forecasting

- Training

- Baseline sales expectations (e.g., sellers only earn variable pay once they meet a performance threshold)

- Compliance (e.g., safety)

Done correctly, the additional fixed cost buys sales organizations a great deal of value from sellers. Additionally, the remaining variable pay plan can be dedicated to pure growth and production measures rather than baseline expectations. One caveat exists. Increased sales supervision is necessary to ensure that the base pay is constantly earned, not given by default.

The trend towards more base-heavy pay mix for distribution field sellers can be a win-win for organizations and sellers. Sales leaders can direct seller activity more effectively. Sales managers can drive more accountability from sellers. And, sellers gain a degree of security through cash flow with only modestly foregoing often hard to achieve stratospheric upside earning opportunities.

Contributing Authors

Craig Ackerman

Matt Bartels

Arshad Carim

David Cichelli

Quang Do

Dave Eddleman

Mitchell Edwards

Priya Ghatnekar

Ted Grossman

Avrille Hanzel

Andrew Horvath

Rachel Parrinello

Chris Semain

Kyle Uebelhor

Igor Uroic

About Alexander Group

The Alexander Group provides revenue growth consulting services to the world's leading sales, marketing and service organizations. Founded in 1985, Alexander Group combines deep experience, proven methodologies and data-driven insights to help revenue leaders anticipate change, align their go-to-customer resources with company goals and make better informed decisions with one goal in mind—to grow revenue. The Alexander Group has offices in Atlanta, Chicago, London, New York, San Francisco, São Paulo, Scottsdale and Vero Beach.

OUR CONSULTING SERVICES

The Alexander Group provides the world's leading revenue acquisition organizations with management consulting services for the full spectrum of sales, marketing and service needs, as well as performance benchmarking based on the industry's richest repository of revenue program performance data. We apply years of experience and our Revenue Growth Model™, a proven methodology for evaluating go-to-customer organizations, to provide insights that are rooted in facts. We not only deliver insights—we understand sales, marketing and service business challenges. We roll-up our sleeves to work alongside our clients, whether they are realigning revenue acquisition programs or radically overhauling their go-to-customer resources. Our keen focus on measurement ensures that we deliver value and results to our clients.

ABOUT ALEXANDER GROUP EVENTS

The Alexander Group produces and facilitates a specialized portfolio of events that help the world's leading revenue teams to drive growth. From our Executive Forum to Executive Roundtables, all events cover topics that range from big-picture strategy to hands-on execution. Participants benefit from connecting with other top sales, marketing and service leaders, and gain exclusive access to the latest ideas and deeper insights needed to create high-performance revenue-growth organizations.

CPSIA information can be obtained
at www.ICGtesting.com
Printed in the USA
LVHW082148290722
724730LV00011B/511